Creative Family Projects,
Games and Activities

CREATIVE FAMILY
PROJECTS, GAMES
AND ACTIVITIES

Cynthia MacGregor

A CITADEL PRESS BOOK
Published by Carol Publishing Group

A Citadel Press Book
Published by Carol Publishing Group
Citadel Press is a registered trademark of Carol Communications, Inc.
Editorial Offices: 600 Madison Avenue, New York, N.Y. 10022
Sales and Distribution Offices: 120 Enterprise Avenue, Secaucus, N.J.
   07094
In Canada: Canadian Manda Group, One Atlantic Avenue, Suite 105,
   Toronto, Ontario M6K 3E7
Queries regarding rights and permissions should be addressed to
Carol Publishing Group, 600 Madison Avenue, New York, N.Y. 10022

Carol Publishing Group books are available at special discounts for
bulk purchases, sales promotions, fund-raising, or educational
purposes. Special editions can be created to specifications. For
details, contact Special Sales Department, Carol Publishing Group,
120 Enterprise Avenue, Secaucus, N.J. 07094

Manufactured in the United States of America
10 9 8 7 6 5 4 3 2 1

Library of Congress Cataloging-in-Publication Data

MacGregor, Cynthia.
   Creative family projects, games and activities / Cynthia MacGregor.
        p.   cm.
   "A Citadel Press book."
   ISBN 0–8065–1636–4
   1. Family recreation.   2. Amusements.   3. Games.   4. Handicrafts.
I. Title
GV182.8.M3   1995
790.1′91—dc20   94–41145
                                                           CIP

For Laurel, Mark, Justin, and Tori...with love.

Contents

8 Just for Fun   181

Family Talent Night / Customized Family Board
Games / Snow Paintings / Rebuses and Similar
Puzzles / Telephone Words / Limericks / Captions
Outrageous / Cow Bingo / Interfamily Competitions /
Puppet Theater / Hot and Cold

9 Miscellaneous Projects   205

Family Bike Hike / Weekly Walk / "Toys R Not Us"
Day / Raising Tropical Fish / Special Events Pig /
This Family Is for the Birds / Photo Collages /
Mixed Media Photo-Drawings / Sandcasting / Rock
Face Paperweights

The author deeply appreciates the invaluable help
of Vic Bobb.

Thanks also to Patrice Levin.

Introduction

"Let's all do something together." How many times have you made that suggestion, or at least had that thought... then come up blank about what the family could do? You *want* to do something with the kids, want to spend some quality time with them... but you're baffled as to what to do.

Of course, you could all play a board game together. But maybe you're looking for a more meaningful way to invest some time in togetherness. Something that will have an impact on your kids' lives. Or something that will produce a tangible result. Or simply something that you'll enjoy more than another round of Candyland.

Maybe you've thought that your family doesn't spend as much time as you'd like on activities *together*. But how many things are there that you—adults and kids alike—can all get into with some enthusiasm? Perhaps you've made a conscious resolution to spend more time actively doing things with your kids. But *what*? It isn't always easy to think of things you'll all enjoy doing.

In fact, not all the activities in this book are simply *fun*—several, to be sure, are quite serious. But they're all worthwhile projects for a family to engage in together. Of course not all families are constructed equally. "Family" can mean Mom and Dad and four kids, or two parents and one child, or one parent and one or more kids. But most of the activities in this book will suit most of the members of most families. And that's a good place to start.

So the next time you think, "Wouldn't it be nice to all do something together," you won't have to wind up shrugging your shoulders and going back to the crossword for lack of inspiration. You've got a bookful of projects your family can embark on—brain-stretchers, educational projects, holiday projects, practical projects, family-oriented projects, serious projects, and, yes, some just-for-fun projects, along with a few I've simply labeled "Miscellaneous."

Remember, too, that you're not just filling hours or strengthening bonds. You're making memories. Memories you'll cherish when you look at your college graduate striding down the aisle, about to receive a diploma, and remember him or her as an eight-year-old helping you compile a Family History. Memories your child will cherish himself or herself, from the vantage point of adulthood, when she or he looks back and remembers not just discipline but love, not just family squabbles but brightly glowing moments when you all shared in a special project, or an ongoing family ritual, a memory to be cherished.

These times of togetherness are some of the concrete blocks upon which a solid family relationship is built. Make them count. And enjoy them.

1

Family Togetherness

Weekly Wrap-up

Materials needed: pen and paper, possibly typewriter or computer

Crowded with so many facts and figures, it's no wonder our minds tend to forget little details, names, facts, dates, and data that seem so important and so obvious now.

Right now you think you'll never forget the name of Johnny's third-grade teacher, the color of his first bike and what year he got it, or the name of Kayla's Girl Scout leader. You know you'll never forget that awful station wagon that turned out to be such a lemon, the one you gave up on after two years and traded in.

But ten or twenty years from now, you're going to be asking yourselves questions like, "When did Kayla cut her hair short?" "What year did I stay up all night making cookies for the bake sale that Johnny forgot to tell me about till the night before?" and other weighty questions of life. And Kayla and Johnny won't remember the answers to the questions, either.

They and you may also have forgotten their music teacher's name, the merit badges they earned in Scouts, and just what was wrong with that awful station wagon. The story of how you transported six Scouts in it, got lost, and never did find the Jamboree may slip from your memory in years to come, too, despite how vividly it replays in your mind now.

That's why you need a Weekly Wrap-up. Think of it as a family journal, a log of the highlights, that will prompt your

3

memories a year from now or a generation later. Whether you need to look up an item for a form you're filling out or the search is a purely pleasurable mental journey through your past, you'll have a recorded log of the highlights of your family's experiences, with requisite hard facts mixed in.

The entries can be as detailed or sketchy as you wish: "Johnny got a red bike, his first two-wheeler, and rode it around the block twice before he fell. He'd been practicing on his friend Jerry's bike" would be sufficient, or you can go into greater detail.

Likewise, "Kayla started fourth grade in the new Eisenhower Elementary. Her teacher is Ms. Harrison" will do, or you can be more specific about which of her friends are in her class this year, which room of the school her class is in, and the fact that there are only twenty-two kids in the class. It's important that you get the basic facts; how much detail you add is up to you.

The family can gather around the dining room table as you write longhand, or around your computer, each putting in his or her own contributions.

Johnny: "I caught five frogs near the pond when we went to visit Grandpa."

Kayla: "I got an *A* on my spelling test, and a best-friend Valentine from Susy."

Dad: "I finished a desk for Johnny in my basement woodshop."

Mom: "I took Kayla to work with me on Friday, when school was closed, so she could see what my office looks like."

It all goes into the record. Like a Sunday news wrap-up, it summarizes the week, preserving the family's world in their own words, keeping memories saved on paper for reminiscing and even for future generations to read.

It's important to establish a regular time for writing the wrap-up and then stick to it. Otherwise you'll start skipping it "just this once," and "this once" will turn into lots of "once"s, and soon the habit will be abandoned totally and the project will die out. Likewise, if you put it off saying, "We'll catch up next week," events of the earlier week will have been overshadowed by more recent ones, and salient bits will get lost.

If you're tempted to succumb to modern technology and videotape the log, I'd caution against it. Yes, seeing your kids (and yourselves) on camera as reporters, covering the week past, is appealing. Yes, the presentation seems more alive than reading from pages of a book. But there are pitfalls, too.

First of all, a book is more accessible. It's easier to get a book out for a quick read than to find the right tape, load it in, and watch little bits of it. It's also easier to find the right place quickly in a book ("Where's Christmas of '94?" "I want to read about the summer of '95") than on a tape.

Then, too, disasters are more apt to occur to a tape— accidental erasure, distortion due to time, mechanical problems with the cassette—than to a book.

And last of all, though camcorders and VCRs were considered to be on the cutting-edge of technology as recently as just a few years ago, in twenty years they may be outmoded, replaced by a newer, better technology. It's hard to find a phonograph on which to play old LPs anymore; in twenty years, when you're ready for a good session of reminiscing through the Weekly Wrap-up family log, you may not have a machine on which to play the tape. But a book—that's always accessible.

If you're terribly eager to tape "news reports" of the family's week, use these as adjuncts to your written reports, not as a replacement for them.

Family Trivia

*Materials needed: a fair number of 3″ × 5″ index
cards, pens, piece of paper for keeping score.
(Optional: A Trivial Pursuit board)*

Though you can play a version of this game somewhat along
the lines of Trivial Pursuit, substituting your own for the board
game's questions, it's not at all necessary. I've provided you with
rules for two simple trivia games that require nothing but index
cards, pens, and a piece of paper for scoring.

Pass out an equal number of cards to each family member;
the exact number is not important, though more is better. Have
each person write one trivia question on each card, with the
answer on the flip side. Questions may refer to the historical
past and family trivia that have been talked of before, such as
"What did Great-Grandpa Evan do for a living?" or "What
country did Grandma Bess's family come from?"

Questions may refer to the present family:

• "What game did we play day after day in the tent, when it
  rained during almost the whole trip to Coffeepot Rapids?"
• "What make and color of car was Uncle Ed driving when
  he came to see us three summers ago?"

Very young family members might ask such questions as:

• "Who was Janie's first-grade teacher?"
• "What part did Les play in the school spring pageant in
  second grade?"

After each person has written the question and answer on the
card, place a large initial of the family's last name on the
question side, so you know which side is to face up if you put all
the cards together (Game 2). Each player, should also initial the

upper left corner of the question side so there is no doubt about which cards originated with which family members.

Game 1

Each person holds his or her own cards and play proceeds in a circle. Each player gets to ask one question of any person present per turn. After asking the question, the questioner places that card at the bottom of his or her own deck. If the questioner stumps the person to whom the question is directed, the questioner gets one point. If the person asked knows the correct answer, she or he gets two points. After ten rounds, the player with the most points wins.

Game 2

The cards are all shuffled and placed in a pile question-side up. Play proceeds in a circle. Each player asks a question of the person to his or her right, drawing the top card and checking first to make sure that that card was not created by the person to be asked. If it was, it is returned to the bottom of the deck and the next card is drawn. A person who answers a question correctly earns a point. There is no score to the questioner for wrong answers. The first player to score ten points wins the game.

Family Time Capsules

Materials needed: a box and various meaningful things to put in it (see below)

A time capsule doesn't have to be literally buried, nor does it have to wait a hundred years to be opened. Why not make a "time capsule" for each of your children, to be opened at an appropriate time in the future.

The capsule should reflect the world as it was the day they were born, and, of course, the best time to make it is literally around the time of each child's birth, or during his or her first year. But even if you already have children, it's not too late to start. Amass the largest possible number of the items listed below, and any others that occur to you as suitable. So what if it's not as complete as if you'd compiled it at the time of birth—it'll still be meaningful when your child is grown and looking back at the way the world was at the time of his or her birth.

What you'll include in the child's time capsule is highly subjective and entirely up to you, but here are a few suggestions:

- A newspaper from the day the child was born, preferably a hometown newspaper, showing news not only of the world but of your hometown. Naturally this is easiest to do on the day the child is born. Yet even if you're putting the capsule together when he or she is eight years old, your local paper may have back issues. Inquire. Failing that, there are newspapers from most dates in recent history available through various mail-order catalogues.
- Magazines from the year the child was born. The ads will show fashions in clothing, hairstyles, cars, and furnishings. They will also reflect prices of the day, which may amaze your child when he or she is grown and looking back at life "way back when." The articles in the magazine will show the general concerns of the day, especially if it's a news magazine, but you'll also want to include a personalities magazine to show who was famous at the time, and perhaps a fashion magazine (men's or women's), and even special-interest magazines. The ads may be as much a revelation eighteen or twenty-one years from now as the articles are. The prices of products advertised, the products themselves, and even the styles of advertising will be of interest.

- Significant articles, such as a pair of the child's infant-sized socks. ("Did my feet really fit in *those*?")
- Photos of yourselves as you looked that year, your child at birth, family pets, siblings, and possibly other significant people in your life.
- A "wish list" of your aspirations for your child. (Not just, "I want him to grow up to be a _____," but what you want out of life for him or her.)
- Photos of your home—whether house or apartment—exterior and interior. Take a picture of every room in the house if possible. Take detailed pictures of the child's room.
- A list of the people who attended the christening, bris, dedication, or other religious ceremony, if any, that you may have had for the child, along with a description, in your own words, of the ceremony and any party that may have followed.
- A written or tape-recorded statement of the feelings of every family member old enough to express himself or herself regarding the arrival of this newest member. It can be brief or long. Each person needs to identify himself or herself before speaking if tape recording.
- A list of all the baby gifts received—including a brief description of the item and the name of the person who gave it.
- The child's favorite toy, provided he or she gives it up early enough that it can be included in the time capsule without being missed—and without your holding the capsule aside for a year, waiting for it. (It will be tempting to keep opening the capsule and adding to it, but, really, it should be put together and sealed shortly after the child's birth, if possible, and then left alone till the date it's due to be opened.)
- Copies of the birth announcement you sent out, of the local newspaper's birth announcement, and of any other

birth announcements (such as in Mom's or Dad's company's newspaper or newsletter, if any).

- The hospital's wristband or anklet worn by the baby.
- A band from the "It's a Boy/Girl" cigars Dad gave out, if he did.
- A copy of the hospital bill for the birth. It may seem like a lot of money now, but by the time your baby is grown, all of you will laugh at how little it cost to get born in "those days."
- A packet of football or baseball cards from that year, showing the major players in the sport at the time. (One of these may even prove highly valuable in years to come.)
- A tape of the infant crying, gurgling, and cooing.
- A footprint and handprint of the newborn child.
- A picture of the baby as drawn by an older sibling.
- Any other items that you feel will give the child a feel for what the world was like at the time of his or her birth. This includes both your immediate world and the world at large: customs, mores, fashions, pastimes, the slang of the day, concerns of the day...all this and more is fair game for inclusion in the capsule.

The "time capsule" itself doesn't have to be anything fancier than a large, sturdy box. You can stow it away on an upper shelf, in the attic, or somewhere else out of reach. Seal it with tape to prevent the temptation of breaking into it ahead of schedule.

Now about that schedule—when should the capsule be opened? Suggested dates include the following. Choose the one that best suits you:

- The child's eighteenth birthday
- The child's twenty-first birthday
- The child's wedding
- The child's high school or college graduation
- The birth of the child's own first child

Grandpa's Pumpkin; Grandma's Valentine

Materials needed: pen and paper or tape and tape recorder, possibly computer or typewriter

Some of the most rewarding family activities are the intergenerational ones, those that put the youngest generation in touch with older generations and get them really involved. Sharing and recording family history is particularly rewarding. It creates a special bond, even beyond the more immediately visible benefits of getting the generations involved with and understanding each other better. And the younger ones get to know what life was like "in the olden days."

Too often, kids lose sight of the true picture of life in even the 1960s or 1940s, let alone the 1920s or the last century. With TV shows full of anachronisms, like the Flintstones watching TV, kids have inaccurate mental pictures of what inventions existed when.

"You mean Great-Great-Grandma didn't even have a telephone?"

"What do you mean, Grandpa didn't have a television when he was my age?"

"No *video games*? What did you *do* when you were a child?"

These are concepts that kids may be slow to pick up on. And if you all live far apart from each other, they have even less opportunity to get to know the generations two or more ahead of them. Sometimes an open-ended question like: "Tell me about life when you were a girl, Grandma" may not elicit a good response, or may result in a story that doesn't hold the grandchild's interest. Specific questions, questions about activities the kids can relate to, have a better chance of succeeding both in the stories they evoke and in the interest these stories generate in the kids.

One fertile field for such questions is the topic of holidays and celebrations. "Tell us how you celebrated Halloween, Grandpa." "What were birthday parties like when you were a girl, Grandma?" "How did your family celebrate Christmas?" "Did you get lots of Valentines when you were a girl?"

Preserving the stories can be accomplished in various ways. For the child adept at writing quickly, or even typing quickly and accurately, the stories can be taken down longhand or on typewriter or computer. Otherwise, since it seems even five-year-olds are handy with cassette recorders these days, the accounts of celebrations past can be taped by the child, to be either transcribed later or simply preserved on tape.

Transcribing them onto paper in some form is recommended, though. Tapes can break or simply deteriorate, and while it's nice having the story preserved in Grandma's or Great-Grandpa's own voice, there is the risk of losing the whole thing. So the best bet is to copy the contents of the tape onto paper, then preserve the tape as well.

It's probably too much to ask relatives to sit down and talk for hours about holidays past, but one way to accumulate your history is to approach the relatives around the time of every holiday. At Christmas, ask such questions as:

- "How did your family celebrate Christmas when you were a kid?"
- "How did the celebration of Christmas differ at the time you were a child from how we celebrate it now?"
- "What are some of the most memorable Christmases of your past?"

At Valentine's Day, appropriate questions might include:

- "Did you buy or make Valentines to send?"
- "Tell me about the first Valentine you sent—not to your family."
- "Tell me about the first Valentine you received—not from your family."

Around Halloween, ask about parties, jack-o'-lanterns, trick-or-treating, pranks, and other ways of celebrating.

Of course, if the relatives live out of town, you and the kids may need to ask your questions whenever you have the opportunity... when the relatives are visiting you, or you're visiting them, regardless of the proximity of holidays. You may even need to interview them by asking questions during a phone call or mailing them lists of questions to answer when they have the time to write at length.

As the seasons and holidays cycle past, the family will accumulate an impressive collection of stories and recollections. Gathering them into a book—loose-leaf or otherwise—will offer hours of fascinating reading to later generations. Some will deal with how things were done in general in the "olden days"; others will be more purely personal... Grandma Ann's own particular way of celebrating Thanksgiving.

Note: Of course there is no reason to confine your questions to holiday memories only. Putting together a book of family holiday reminiscences is a wonderful special project, and holiday customs are a great place to start when you're looking for specific areas to ask about. But all other storytelling and recollections are of equally inestimable value. See elsewhere in this book for other approaches to preserving family history and memories.

Write a Family History

Materials needed: pen and paper, and preferably a typewriter or computer as well

I'm sure your kids know where you were born; they probably know whether and where you went to college, and they might even know what country your ancestors emigrated from. But do they know:

- What your early career aspirations were?
- Where all four of their grandparents were born?
- How and where their own parents—you two—met?

In short, while they've been studying world, national, and local history in school, how much do they know about *family* history?

- Did Dad have another career before his present one?
- What about Mom? Whether she's a lawyer or a homemaker now, in what field did she work when she first got out of school?
- Which relatives "came over" from "the old country"—and what was "the old country"?
- Was it the same on both sides of the family...or do you have ancestors from four different countries, some of whose own ancestors, in turn, came from other countries?

If the kids know their grandparents well, they probably know what Grandma's and Grandpa's occupations are or were. But if their grandparents are retired or live in a different city, or if they are no longer living, how much do the kids know about them?

- Do they know whether Grandpa was a butcher or a bus driver, a doctor, a plumber, or a watch-repair specialist?
- Do they know whether Grandma had a career of her own and, if so, what it was?
- Do they know much about Grandma and Grandpa's childhoods, hometowns, siblings, schooling, talents, and accomplishments?
- And how much do they know about their great-grandparents and beyond?

Assuming Grandma and Grandpa on both sides of the family are still alive, the kids (and you, too) can interview them for a family history. Even if the grandparents are living across the continent, they can answer questions, either by phone or by mail.

If any of your kids are thinking of becoming writers, this is good interviewing practice. Even if they have no such aspirations, though, they shouldn't be put off by the thought of the interview... after all, they're talking to their own grandparents.

Compile as exhaustive or brief a family history as you care to, depending also on how much information is available. If your family has been in this country for five or six generations, available information about where they emigrated from, and what kind of life your ancestors had in the old country, may be minimal. If, on the other hand, your own grandparents are still around, and it was their parents who came to the United States, you may be able to get detailed information about life in Ireland, Sweden, Russia, India, South Africa, Italy, or wherever.

You may not know as much as you'd like to about your own family, either. Now's your chance—jump in and ask questions yourselves; or if the kids are handling all the interviewing of grandparents, suggest to them some questions you yourselves would like the answers to.

But surely you also can be a good source of information, if only about your own past, your own childhood, birthplace, education, and the like. And chances are you know a lot about your parents and their backgrounds, including what the family's name was in "the old country," if different than it is now, or what the maiden names were down the female lines. The family history you compile can be as brief or as exhaustive as you wish, limited only by the amount of information that's available.

Once you have all the information, put it into some kind of durable format. The simplest is to type it all up on loose-leaf paper (or on your computer, leaving enough of a left-hand margin for you to hole-punch the paper afterward). Then you can store the pages in a loose-leaf binder for posterity. Many other formats are possible, depending on how much material you've gathered, how fancy you want the final format to be, and how much artistic ability your family has. But the emphasis here is on gathering the information and storing it for posterity, rather than on a fancy presentation.

Note: If you happen to be divorced, don't make light of the other side of the family. Even if kids don't live with both parents, they ought to know about both sides of the family. It took two parents, two sets of genes, two sides of the family to create your children, and their history is that of both of you. Encourage them to dig up information from both sides.

Draw Your Family Tree

Materials needed: pen and large piece of paper

At the same time you're compiling your family history (see above), it's a good idea to also get all the information you need to draw a family tree. It's a part of your family history, and it will also help unconfuse the kids if they can't quite get it straight how Cousin Bobby is related, or to which branch of the family Uncle Lou belongs.

Family relationships can be hard to keep straight, especially in large families with many branches, or in today's spread-out families, where many relatives are mere names to kids who have never met them, or have met them once at best. And if Great-Aunt Myra isn't called that, but simply Aunt Myra, or if Cousin Artie is older than Uncle Matt, or if there's both a Cousin Jerry and an Uncle Jerry, it's awfully easy for the kids, especially the little ones, to get confused.

You need a large piece of paper, and you need to write small, though not so small that it's discouraging or difficult to try to read. Include as many branches as will fit on the paper; draw separate trees for some of the branches, if necessary. (If Dad's sister's husband's brother and his wife, and their kids, are always part of family gatherings, you want to include them for the kids' edification, but there may not be room on the main tree.)

If there's room, and you have the information, you can include year of birth, year of marriage, and year of death where appropriate; if you don't want to get that elaborate, the main thing is just to show who the family members are and how they're related. Once you've explained to the kids how to "read" a family tree, seeing it on paper will make the interconnections of family relationships a lot easier to understand than just hearing "Cousin Laurie is married to Seth; he's Rita and Al's son; Rita is Daddy's sister."

Draw a Family Timeline

Materials needed: a long piece of paper, pen

For this one, you're going to need at least one *l-o-o-o-n-g* piece of paper. You can tape a number of sheets of typing paper or construction paper end to end, or you can ask your local newspaper for some newsprint from the end of a roll, or ask a local merchant with brown wrapping paper in long rolls (such as an independent butcher might have) for a long strip... or two or three. (Why two or three? Because you might want to draw more than one timeline, and because you might mess up the first time and want to start over on a fresh piece of paper.)

There are several ways to approach this project.

- You can draw a timeline with just your immediate family on it.

- You can draw a timeline that goes back several generations.
- You can include only family events on it.
- You can include world and national news events, too. (If Mom was born the year JFK was shot, that gives Caitlin something to peg each of these events on and makes the year of both events more meaningful to her. Young ones, especially, tend to think of FDR's time as ancient history, almost as far back as the fall of Ancient Rome!)
- You can draw parallel timelines, one showing family events and the other showing events that took place in the world at large at the same time.

Let's start with the simplest timeline first, one of your immediate family. You may want to use a two-colored system, though that's not necessary. Draw a straight horizontal line, marking off every five years in equal increments. Start the timeline over on the left-hand edge of the paper, with a vertical mark representing the beginning of the decade in which your wedding took place. In other words, if you were married in 1984, your family's timeline would start with 1980, represented by a vertical mark. Label it.

Now mark off 1985 and 1990 and label them. If you're reading this after 1995, you should mark and label that year, too. Leave plenty of room at the right for more years. And do all this in one color—say, black.

Now, in red, mark a vertical line for each event in your family. A line inserted in red at the appropriate point for 1984 would be labeled (still in red) "1984. Mom & Dad married." Another line would read "1986. Jenny born." Another line, at 1988, would read, "1988. Max born." You might want a line reading "1992. Jenny starts elementary school." And so forth.

A more comprehensive—and compressed—timeline could go back several generations or even a century. It would show such events as: "1880. Great-Great-Great-Grandma Mary arrives from Germany." "1901. Great-Great-Grandpa Lou born." "1958. Great-Great-Grandma Ross dies." "1959. Grandma and Grandpa O'Donnell get married." "1960. Dad born." In cases such as these, it's best to stick to immediate forebears—parents, grandparents, great-grandparents, and further back if desired, omitting great-aunts, cousins, and so forth.

On that same timeline, preferably in yet a different color, or else on a parallel timeline immediately below it, you can show major world events:

- "World War I ends."
- "Great Depression starts."
- "World War II starts."
- "JFK assassinated."

The above time markers are certainly items you'll want to include if your timeline encompasses the years for all these happenings. How many others, and which ones, you'll include is up to you.

Likewise, what other family events you'll include beyond immigrations, births, deaths, and marriages is entirely up to you. This will depend in part on the size of your family, how far back you're drawing your timeline, and how many events there have been. Divorces, if any, are a good candidate for inclusion. If any family member received a signifcant honor or had a major accomplishment, consider putting that on the timeline as well:

- "Grandpa Larry's play produced."
- "Dad gets his picture in national magazine."
- "Family goes to Disney World."

This last is suitable for inclusion if the trip was a major event in the kids' lives, a once-in-a-lifetime trip.

A Family Timeline will help the kids get a better grasp of family history and a better comprehension of how one event relates to another, time-wise. Drawing events of importance in the larger world, and showing them in relationship to family events, will help kids better understand recent history, too.

Digging for Roots
Down Memory Lane

Materials needed: none other than possibly your car, for traveling

It's important for kids to understand that Mom and Dad were once children, too, going through many of the same heartaches and hassles, joys and disappointments, highs and lows, excitements and disasters that they, the kids, are now experiencing.

Mom was once a girl who disappointed her parents with some of her report card grades, hated a teacher or two, went through the excitement and agonies of first dates and other milestones, and fell and scraped her knee roller-skating.

Dad, too, went through the triumphs and tragedies that accompany childhood—a pet that died, a best friend who moved away, a turn-down from the football team, the winning sixth-grade essay, top prize in the fourth-grade candy sale, the sheer joy of getting on his first bike without training wheels, pushing off, and soaring.

But it's hard for kids to think of their parents as ever being young, ever being kids, ever undergoing the same experiences the kids are now going through themselves. One way to help them connect with this knowledge is a visit to Mom's and Dad's old neighborhoods, whether those are in the same town the kids are growing up in or clear across the continent.

Even when a family still lives in the town where both parents grew up, it's ironic how many parents never think to take their kids back to the old neighborhood. It helps the kids connect if the parents can show them as many of the landmarks of their childhoods as are still in existence.

And if you grew up a thousand miles away from where you're raising your kids, a trip "back home" is worthwhile even if you no longer have any family there to visit. Perhaps you can make a side trip to your old hometown in the course of a family car trip to some other destination.

If Mom and Dad didn't both grow up in the same place, visit one hometown during one year's travels and the other on another occasion. Or dedicate your summer vacation one year to revisiting old haunts and make the trip down memory lane the focus of your summer travels.

But whether you grew up across town or across the country, you need to point out the landmarks of your everyday life, along with the sites of highlights, to your kids:

"You know that little scar on my knee? This is the swing I fell off that's the cause of that scar."

"This is where your Uncle Eddy and I used to go fishing."

"This is the vacant lot where we used to play ball."

"This is the store where my sister and I used to go get milk when Mom ran out between trips to the supermarket."

"This is the dead-end street where we all played touch football."

"Here's right where I was standing when I got my first kiss."

Your children's sense of the two of you as "real people" with lives like their own and interesting experiences will be heightened by your showing them as many of the locales of your childhood as you can. Is your old school still standing? Take them there. If you can get inside, so much the better, but even if you can't show them your fourth-grade classroom or your high school homeroom, show them the outside of the school, the playground, the ball field if there is one and you played on it.

Show them the stores where you shopped. Who knows—Mr. Brown may still be the proprietor of the candy store, even now...or his daughter may have taken over and be running what is still a family business, and may be thrilled to hear you reminisce about her dad's days behind the counter.

Go back to your old house, too. At the very least, you can point out the window of your old room, your mom's favorite rosebush, and the raised spot in the concrete where your sister tripped and dropped the eggs, breaking all twelve of them. But do ring the doorbell. When you explain why you're there, the current owners may be gracious enough to let you in to look around.

If they don't, it's understandable, of course. The house may not be presentable for company; the new owners may be concerned about the safety of letting strangers in their house, too. But you have nothing to lose by asking, and you may be pleasantly surprised by a warm welcome and an invitation to come in and look around.

The new owners may also be interested to know the family history that occurred within those walls. "One year, we were having the house repainted inside, and Mom said we could choose our own colors for our rooms. I chose a hideous shade of green. It looked great on the color chart but awful on the walls, and I had to live with it. After two years, Mom finally relented and let me repaint it myself. I was fourteen by then, and my friends wouldn't let me hear the last of it about that color. I conned three of them into helping me with the repainting." Stories like that bring the past to life for your kids and may be tales you've never thought of telling till prompted by the sight of that room.

Hearing you tell about your past will also encourage the kids to pass along stories of *their* childhoods, in years to come, when they're the parents, and will keep the thread of continuity of generations intact, preserving family history down through the years. The stories you told them will be more vivid for their having seen the sites where the incidents, or everyday happenings, occurred, and your family history, along with their own, will be passed along in the time-honored oral tradition.

Highway to the Past

Materials needed: none

This is a good game for a long car trip. It takes up lots of time while giving the kids a chance to hear about family history, and it also gives them a chance to challenge you.

As you travel down the road, whether it's a country lane, a superhighway, or a local street, each child in turn, starting with the youngest, picks any feature you pass and calls it out, for example "moving van," "barn," "skyscraper," "blue jay," "maple tree," "mailbox," depending on the surroundings and on what thing you've passed that she or he thinks is most apt to stump you.

The parent or parents in the car now have to come up with a story from either their own past or from larger family history that revolves around that object—not that *particular* barn or blue jay, of course—and tell the story to the kids. It could be of how Grandpa Jerry's dad painted the barn orange, and why; or of how you and your friends raced up the stairs of a forty-story building on a dare, and how you won not only by being one of only three out of ten to make it all the way to the top but being the first to get there. Each parent in the car has to come up with a story that centers around the called-out object. If he or she can't, the child who called the object gets a point.

After the youngest child has called out an object, and each parent has had a chance to respond or default, the next-to-youngest child has a turn. Children are allowed to call only objects that they actually spot as you pass them (this could include pictures on billboards). Parents cannot make stories up; they have to be actual occurrences.

If you have only one child traveling with you, the goal is to see how many points he or she can rack up. With two or more kids in the family, it becomes a competition, with each child trying to get the most points by stumping Mom or Dad the most often. (You may want to decide in advance how many rounds you'll play before tallying up the score, or you may want to take it as it comes, ending the game when you get to your destination or when the kids grow restless and it's time to try something else.)

If you have two families traveling together in the car, you can make it an interfamily competition, with all the Johnsons, kids and parents alike, calling out items for the Richardses—kids as well as parents—to tell stories about, and vice versa. The younger kids are likely to come up with very short stories ("I saw a blue jay on the way to school and threw it a corner of my sandwich, but it flew away"), but they'll enjoy participating.

Picture Perfect

Materials needed: family photos; album(s) to hold them; felt-tipped, fine-point, permanent marker; three large boxes

Ready for a pop quiz? (And you thought you were free of those dreaded demons once you graduated from school!) Quick—take out the family photo albums, both those of your current-generation family, and those you may be holding from generations gone by. Open to an early page of your this-generation-family's album...maybe one showing your now-twelve-year-old daughter at age four.

See the girl with the raspberry ice cream smeared all over her face, standing next to your daughter? Her nursery school best friend, right? What was the name of that girl? Where was the picture taken? The two girls were four years old then, right...or were they five?

Now turn to the album of your ancestors. That man standing next to Grandpa Harrison...who is he? His brother? His neighbor? His lodge brother? A visiting army buddy? See the interesting-looking house behind them? Was that Grandpa Harrison's house? (Too bad he's not around anymore for you to ask.)

You may have forgotten your daughter's nursery school best friend's name. But even if do remember it, are you sure you still will in another ten years? And, in years to come, when *her* children are looking over these photos, will she remember and be able to tell them? Or will the subjects of all thoese photos, and the circumstances surrounding them, be as mysterious to generations to come as the picture of Grandpa Harrison is to you?

Label those photos! It needn't be a chore...in fact, labeling pictures can be a most enjoyable family activity.

Gather around the dining room table (or some similar suitable location) with the pictures, an album to put them in if they're not already stored in one (or several of them, depending on just how many photos we're talking about here), and a felt-tipped permanent marker.

You want the pen felt-tipped so you don't harm the pictures when you bear down to write; a ball point is hard on photos. You want it fine-point so you can write small and compress plenty of explanation onto the back of each picture. And you want it permanent so the ink doesn't run, losing data at very least and damaging pictures at worst.

If the photographs are already stored in an album, remove them one at a time, labeling and returning them. If they're loose in a cardboard box or sitting in their original packets from wherever you got them developed, now's the time to decide which pictures are "keepers," labeling and arranging them in an album. (Don't throw out the rest of the photos. There are several activities elsewhere in this book that make use of the discards.)

Not only is going over the pictures and labeling them a delightful project on its own, but it will provide an equally enjoyable family activity for years and for generations to come—that of looking through the pictures of generations gone by, times gone by, and reliving family history by reading the accompanying data.

Choose the person in the family with the neatest, smallest handwriting to be the Official Labeler. If the quantity of photos to be gone through is large, don't let it daunt you; it can be an activity that takes place in stages, sorting through some photos today and labeling the keepers, then doing more on the next rainy Sunday, and more on a dull evening the next week, and so on till they're done.

As the family gathers around, a good deal of reminiscing is likely to take place: "I remember! We'd gotten lost, and Dad stopped to ask directions at a roadside blueberry stand. We bought a box of blueberries and got blue juice all over the front seat of the car. Our faces got blue, too, and that's when you took the picture. That was on our drive to see Aunt Edna in Iowa."

Take your time. Reminisce. Enjoy the memories. And when nobody is piping up with more recollections, distill the memories into a brief description that hits all the salient points and write that information on the back of the photo. Be careful not to stack the photo back on top of another till you're sure the ink is dry, though, or the consequences could be disastrous.

If the stock of pictures needing to be labeled is particularly large, and if the pictures are not already in albums, get three large boxes. All the unlabeled pictures can be unceremoniously dumped into the first box at the outset. The rejects, to be used for other activities, go in the second box. And the third is for the photos that have been sorted and labeled and are ready to be put in albums. As the stock in the first box diminishes, and the quantity in the third grows steadily, you'll see tangible proof of your progress, even if the project stretches out over many weeks.

One reason that it's important to have the whole family

together as this photographic record of your family's history is labeled is that everyone is likely to have his or her own memory of the events depicted. Bud may remember the blueberry photo as taking place on the trip to the Grand Canyon, and you, not remembering for sure, might be tempted to accept his word for it. But Artie's memory might be better, and he might recall that the incident in question was on the trip to Iowa, providing anecdotal evidence that he's right. Not only will the whole family enjoy the reminiscences that ensue, but you'll get the facts right. And Tina may be the one who remembers the fact that when you stopped off at Cousin Sue's house along the way, there were still some blueberries left, and Sue made a pie out of them.

Some members of the family will know that if the picture was taken in front of the yellow house with the white shutters, the year had to be somewhere between 1985 and 1991. Others may be able to pinpoint the year or place the picture was taken by looking at hairstyles, clothes, people in the photos, or other evidence.

The more information you can cram on the back of that picture, the better, and the more your memory will be able to be jogged to supply still more relevant details in times to come. At minimum, each photo should be labeled with year taken (with a question mark following, if you're not sure), names of people pictured, occasion if any, location if possible, and any other pertinent information you can think of.

And do label the back of the photos, rather than the pages of the album. True, there's more room to write on the pages, if it's the type of album on which one can write. But photos can come loose from their mountings, and once the pictures are separated from their labeled pages—especially years from now—it may be difficult to match up the pictures with their original locations in the book.

Arranging the photos into albums can be a whole other project. If you have a large collection, you may have to break them down into different albums. How you do it is entirely up to you. It can be chronological, with all the pictures in order, and one book picking up where the previous, filled book left off. Or you can do it by subject: birthday parties, Christmases, other relatives, pets, and so on. Or some other system may appeal to you even more. There's no one "right" way—it's whatever works best for your own collection, your own purposes.

But it's important not to treat this project as a chore. Don't plow through it, doggedly determined to get all those photos labeled. Don't make it into work. It should be a fun, relaxed, evening of remember-whens. If it takes three months to complete the sorting and labeling, so be it. It'll be three months of good times together with the family.

Bonus Photo-Labeling Activity

Materials needed: family photos, paper, typewriter or computer if available, otherwise pen

So you're finally labeling all those old photos (see Picture Perfect, above). What a wealth of memories you're all dredging up...a veritable treasure of verbal pictures to go with the actual photos. They're relevant, they're important to you...and there's just too much to fit it all on the backs of the photos.

The photo-labeling project can, if you want, blend right into the next project on your agenda, writing histories of the events depicted in the photos. You can do both simultaneously, or the history writing can take place after the photos are labeled.

The advantage of doing them simultaneously is that the

history writer feeds on the information being supplied as the family reminiscences and writes the histories down right then. If everyone has to go through the process again, on a second occasion, they're likely to skimp on the details for the second go-around.

The advantage of doing them separately, on the other hand, is that you can go through the pictures faster if you're not waiting for the history recorder to get it all down on paper, at much greater length than what someone is writing on the backs of the photos.

Copies of the written account can be made and stored with the pictures, as a sort of elaboration on the labeling. Since the histories relate directly to the pictures, it's logical to keep them together. The histories spin out, in greater detail than the labels have room for, the story behind the story, the details of what went on around the scene that's captured for all time in the photo in the album. And by the same token, the pictures are there to serve as illustrations for the story—sort of an illustrated family history.

Don't neglect to keep up the labels-and-histories as future rolls of pictures get developed. And don't forget to take out the albums and pore over them from time to time, all of you gathered around to look at the pictures and remember times past.

Family Song

Materials needed: pen and paper

When I went to camp as a child, one of the highlights of the summer was the annual Sing, with the camp divided into teams, each team responsible for writing three songs: an alma mater, a march, and a comedy or "pep" song.

The pep songs consisted of many verses, some no more than a

few lines each. Each verse was set to the already-existing tune of a popular song of the day or of a past era.

When possible, we picked songs whose original themes related to the topic of that particular verse. For example, a verse about the counselors having trouble rousing sleeping kids might have been set to the tune of "Oh, What a Beautiful Morning," or "Oh, How I Hate to Get Up in the Morning," or even to "Reveille" itself.

Often, though, there was no correlation between the topic of the original song and that of the verse we were setting to music. We simply selected a catchy tune to which we could easily fit words about the situation we wanted to write about.

If one or more members of your family have a way with words, why not do something similar—a song of multiple verses, celebrating the foibles and peculiarities of your family:

- Did Bob fall out of a tree he was climbing when he was trying to impress a friend with his athletic abilities?
- Does Maureen change clothes seventeen times every morning before she settles on an outfit to wear to school?
- Did Joel, determined not to speed with his new driver's license, get a ticket for going too *slowly*?
- Do Mom's cakes invariably fall?
- Did Rover rob the steaks from the grill the night Dad's boss was the guest at dinner?
- Did Dad whip up a pot of his extra-special chili one night...and totally forget to add any of the spices?

These are all potential topics for verses of the song.

As an alternative, if your kids are into rap and are also wordsmiths, they can write a rap song about the family, its more humorous foibles and peculiarities, and the funniest of the incidents that have occurred over the years...including some that may not have seemed funny at the time.

This can be a total-family project, or the kids can write the song without parental help, then perform it for you one evening.

Postcard Log

Materials needed: postcards (collected wherever the family travels), large box to store them in

One of the most colorful and entertaining ways of preserving memories of a family trip is a postcard log, The log is actually a large box in which the postcards can be stored in some neat manner. (Since you're going to be writing on the backs, pasting them into an album won't work. Using stamp hinges, available anywhere stamp collectors' supplies are sold, to paste them in is a possibility, but keeping them loose is preferable.)

Postcards are the answer if no one in the family is a good photographer. Or if your pictures didn't all come out right. And even if you do take good pictures, postcards can capture additional scenes, pictures you might not have had the opportunity to snap.

Another factor is that, while most of us are reluctant to write on the back of a picture for fear of ruining it, no one's afraid of writing on a postcard. So, since the backs of these pictures are definitely going to be written on, postcards are the obvious solution.

The procedure is both simple and inexpensive. During the course of a family trip, designate a certain amount of money for the specific purpose of purchasing picture postcards memorializing the trip. These postcards might feature scenery, local attractions, historical sites, activities, or whatever you find appealing about the area you're traveling in. And by "traveling" I mean any trip at all—an excursion from the suburbs into the city can even qualify as a trip on which to buy postcards, if such a trip isn't a commonplace occurrence in your family.

Each member of the family who's old enough to hold even a

semisensible opinion can have input into which postcards to purchase. The writing should be done while you're still traveling and the memories and impressions are freshest.

Each night—or whatever works in the context of your time schedule and how frequently you're acquiring postcards—the family should sit down together and go over the postcards you've acquired but have not yet written on. Discuss what impressions or memories you associate with the scenery on each postcard, or with the trip in general if the scene doesn't evoke a specific association.

You can let the person with the most meaningful thoughts write on the postcard, sharing the honor as different people come up with the most trenchant throughts for various postcards. Or the family member with the smallest, neatest handwriting can be the official scribe, recording the impressions regardless of whose thoughts they are.

When you get home, add the postcards from that trip to the others in your collection. You'll probably want to keep each trip or location separated from the others, using a rubber band or even a folder for each group. If your trip of the summer of 1994 involves visits to three different cities, you'll want to decide whether to keep all the postcards together under "Summer of '94" or separate Washington, D.C., Annapolis, and Historic Williamsburg.

However you preserve the postcards, and however you separate them, you'll wind up with a large and growing collection of memories preserved in words and pictures, ready for reminiscing at a moment's notice. The postcards alone would be wonderful souvenirs of your family's trip; with the addition of your personalized comments and recollections, your log becomes a true treasure.

You'll be amazed at how vividly your family's postcard log brings back clear and specific recollections of the trip, whether it's memories of the beauty of natural splendors or of Ryan falling into the motel's swimming pool with all his clothes on.

The written words will couple with the pictures to make them all the more meaningful and evocative.

And gathering around the dining room table with the postcard log on an otherwise dull evening, reviewing trips past, is another delightful family activity, one that can occupy many enjoyable hours.

A "Coat" Without Buttons

Materials needed: pen and paper, more paper and paint

While "official" coats of arms are handed down from generation to generation, there's no reason for you not to create an unofficial one, based on symbols of what is important or relevant about your family.

To decide what those things are, the family needs to get together and discuss just what you'd want to memorialize in your family's coat of arms. Brainstorm. Take notes. Freely spout out ideas of what's important to, relevant to, or illustrative of this family.

Once ideas have been generated and noted, it's time to discuss them:

- Which of these ideas can be illustrated in some form or represented in a word or two?
- Which ones truly denote attributes this family wants to be known for?
- Is "Patience" the family motto?
- Are you all incurable optimists, for whom rays of sunshine would be appropriately emblematic?
- Do you own a farm—would stalks of wheat be appropriate?

- Have you spawned three generations of teachers—would books, or an apple, be appropriate (and if so, which)?

Disagreements will ensue, but they needn't take the form of arguments. (If your kids don't know how to disagree civilly, here's another chance for them to practice!)

As the discussion progresses, you'll likely get into talking over which of the family's characteristics, mottos, traits, and habits are truly significant features of the family's identity and which may loom large now but are not of ultimate importance. You'll come to see more clearly just what the family's goals, beliefs, strengths, and ideals are.

As you refine your list of characteristics, traits, and historical events that might go on your coat of arms, you'll keep shortening the list till you have just the few that are most important and will fit. Now you need to devise ways of representing these:

- Should stalks of wheat or ears of corn represent your farming heritage?
- How many stalks or ears do you want?
- Where on the coat of arms do you want the family byword, "Persevere," to appear?

Once you're agreed on the final form of the coat of arms, have the most artistic member of the family draw the finished product. If you're really into this, but no one in the family has artistic talent, roughly sketch out what you want the coat of arms to look like, then take the sketch to a local artist and let him or her make up the final version.

If you're really caught up in this, you could even incorporate the coat of arms into your stationery, though you certainly want to avoid looking pretentious. Still, there's no sin in being proud of your family and what it represents!

Even if you never go further than designing the coat of arms—never draw it and frame it and hang it, or use it on envelopes or other stationery—creating it will have provided a pleasant part-of-an-afternoon and will have made all of you more conscious of family values and heritage, and just what your family is all about.

Time to Grow

Materials needed: large piece of sturdy cardboard, scissors, marker, and paste or glue; or wood, jigsaw, paint, and glue

How do you display your kids' school pictures? Do you keep them in an album, or display them on your wall cluttered into a frame? Or perhaps you display the current one on your fridge, displacing each picture when the next one becomes available?

Here's an idea: Cut a large circle either out of heavy, sturdy cardboard or, if you have a jigsaw (or have a friend who has one), out of wood. Now draw small clock-style numbers, 1 through 12, in the appropriate places on the circle. Use a marker if drawing on cardboard; use paint on wood.

You probably order an assortment of school pictures every year. Cut just the face out of one picture of each child for each of the grades she or has been through so far and paste it on the appropriate "time" on the clock face: around the *1* place each child's first-grade picture, around the *2* place the second-grade pictures, and so on through *12* for the senior year of high school.

When your youngest graduates from high school, your "clock" will be complete. (Then you can look forward to doing the same thing with your grandchildren's school pictures in a few more years!)

Who Am I—Family Version

Materials needed: pen, paper, safety pin

In the traditional version of Who Am I, a piece of paper is pinned to a player's back. On the paper is written the name of a person, real or fictional, living or dead. The player now has to guess if he or she is Snow White, Queen Elizabeth, Daffy Duck, Roy Rogers, Peter Pan, your next-door neighbor, or some other personage known to all players. He or she does this by asking questions that can be answered with a yes or no: "Am I a real person?" "Am I alive now?" "Am I female?" "Do I live in this town?" And so on.

In the family version, the identity to be guessed is that of a family member, past or present. It could be Great-Grandma Louise, Cousin Eddie, or Mom. It must be someone whose identity is familiar to all the kids, though.

Questions might run along these lines:

- "Am I alive now?"
- "Am I female?"
- "Do I have kids?"
- "Do I have four kids?"
- "Do I live in South Dakota?"
- "Am I known in the family for making fudge with M&Ms in it?"
- "Am I Aunt Jenny?"

Depending on the ages of your kids, you can:

- Make it a Twenty-Question game, with the kids winning if they guess the person in twenty questions and losing if they fail to.
- Make it open-ended, letting them win if they guess it at all, but with the round ending if they make a wrong guess.

- Make it more directly competitive by counting the
  number of questions everyone takes to guess "their"
  identity and declaring the one who guesses in the fewest
  questions the winner.

Variation

Each player decides who she or he wants to be for the game,
keeping it to himself or herself. Others then ask the questions:

- "Are you male?"
- "Were you born in the last century?"
- "Did you fight in World War I?"
- "Were you wounded in the leg?"
- "Are you Great-Great-Grandpa Cohen?"

Here, you can declare as winner the guesser who first comes
up with the right identity, but anyone making a wrong guess is
out of the round.

And if kids start asking questions about family members as a
result of the game, *don't* say, "Not now, we're playing a game."
Take a break. Delve into family history. If they don't know why
Aunt Edna won that award, or why Uncle Al had a hospital
named after him, or the funny story about Cousin Gertie sitting
in the lemon meringue pie at the Fourth of July picnic, by all
means fill them in.

The game will wait.

A Journal for Grandma

*Materials needed: paper and pen or pencil
(or typewriter or computer)*

A journal is not the same as an autobiography (see Illustrated Autobiographies, page 66), nor is it necessarily the same as a diary. A journal *can* contain one's innermost thoughts, like a diary, but more often it's a more mundane recording of the day's or week's events. These journals deal with day-to-day occurrences, rather than simply hitting the highlights. And they are not just for the kids' own future reminiscing, though they'll serve in that capacity in the future, too, but for the more immediate purpose of keeping Grandma (or Grandpa, or Aunt Janet, or some other relative) up-to-date on the day-to-day lives of the kids.

Such famous personages as Nathaniel Hawthorne, Jane Addams, Henry David Thoreau, Mark Twain, and Queen Victoria kept journals. In fact, they've all been published, and if you want to get a feel for the flavor of a journal, you can probably check at least some of these volumes out of your local public library.

A preschool child can start a journal if Mom or Dad acts as secretary, taking down the words in written form. A first-grader may still need lots of help; by second grade, a child should be able to basically write his or her own journal, as long as Mom or Dad (or an older sibling) is nearby to help with the spelling of difficult words.

It doesn't matter whether Grandma (or whoever) lives around the corner or halfway around the world; she'll enjoy getting a record of her grandchild's daily life, including highlights of the school day, the building of a snow fort, enjoyment of a new tree house, sewing a new dress for a doll, the first day in the school band, or a description of every ingredient in the seven-layer sandwich the child invented, created, and ate with gusto (despite Mom's astonishment at the odd combination).

In the process, the child will delight Grandma, assure close contact between them, get into the habit of daily (or weekly) recording and reflecting, and establish a permanent record of activities, growth, thoughts, trials, and triumphs.

The activity is simple—the child simply agrees to devote fifteen minutes a day, let's say, or forty-five minutes a week, to keeping the journal. (Those numbers are arbitrary—feel free to adjust them to suit your own family's reality.) If there are two or more kids in the family, they can all gather to work on their journals, or each can work at a time that's convenient for him or her. Then, at the end of each week, or each month, the journal or journals are hand delivered to Grandma, or packed up and sent.

If Grandma doesn't live nearby, the journal will keep her abreast of her grandchild's activities more extensively yet less expensively than a long distance phone call (although the journals by no means replace the sound of the child's voice at the other end of the phone line). But even if Grandma lives next door, the journal provides a permanent record of her grand-child's childhood, one she can re-read with great pleasure whenever she wants.

And, of course, years later, when Ed and Ann are grown, they can temporarily retrieve the journals from Grandma, go back and re-read them, and enjoy reliving their earlier years (though a certain amount of dismay or embarrassment will be inevitable at some of the entries!).

Just think how much you yourself would enjoy being able to relive select passages of your own childhood. Think how much you might enjoy browsing through handwritten (or typed) accounts of your own early years—or of your parents'.

Your children, and their children and grandchildren, will be

able to finger-walk through their childhoods, stopping at selected spots and recapturing the emotions of memorable "firsts"
and other select occasions. Birthday parties, family trips, class
experiences and everyday joys, sorrows, and happenings will all
be there in writing, preserved for posterity.

"Gee—I'd forgotten that surprise party!"

"Oh, wow—remember when I did laundry for the first time,
threw in my purple skirt, and turned Dad's socks lilac!"

"I'd forgotten Jeff. And he was my best friend in first grade
and the beginning of second, till his family moved."

"Do you remember the year it snowed for Halloween, and we
made snow ghosts and witches on the front lawn? I'd forgotten."

"Here's where I fell in the brook and then you slipped and fell
in helping me out."

You can't make the past yield up something that doesn't exist,
but you can make sure that when the present becomes the past,
you've got a written record of it, one that Grandma can enjoy
now, and the kids can borrow back to enjoy later.

The inevitable strengthening of the connection between the
kids and Grandma is another benefit derived from their keeping
journals. Intimacy grows from the kids' sharing their lives on a
steady, regular basis. At first there may be awkwardness: "I
don't know what to write." "Nothing happened today." But with
time, the kids will grow used to the journals and will more
easily record the events and even thoughts of their lives.

Some days, there may be nothing worth recording; for a child
whose life is not particularly filled with exciting activities, a
weekly setting-down of events may suffice. But a child's life
doesn't have to be filled with birthday parties, ballet recitals, or
playing tricks on a substitute teacher to be exciting. Simply
finding a snail on a sidewalk or counting twenty worms between
the house and the corner after a rain are newsworthy events to
an eight-year-old.

So are making a new friend, or seeing the first robin of the
spring or the first gold-colored leaf of fall or the first Christmas

decorations of the season on the ride to school one autumn day. As the child grows, the events and thoughts recorded will change in nature, but Grandma's delight will assuredly remain constant.

This Day in Pictures

Materials needed: paper, crayons or colored markers (or colored chalk or other medium)

Besides A Journal for Grandma (above), another charming way to keep a small child in touch with his or her grandma, grandpa, aunt, uncle, or other relative is to establish the practice of the child drawing one picture at the end of every day. The picture should be the child's record of his or her day's most prominent event or of impressions of the day as a whole. One picture is not a lot to ask of a child—not like asking him or her to do extra homework or a really tedious, onerous chore.

And for kids too young to write or spell well, a picture is the ideal solution for keeping in touch, although drawing a picture doesn't have to be a replacement for keeping a journal. A child can do both, or keep the journal for Grandma and draw daily pictures for Aunt Irene.

A caption helps explain the picture to Grandma, or whoever. If the child is too young to write, the explanation of the picture can be dictated to Mom or Dad. It doesn't have to be lengthy. It's fine if it's something simple like, "Billy and I made Native American jewelry in Crafts Club today, after school. I gave him mine and he gave me his. We're best friends." Or "There's a new girl in nursery school. Her family just moved here from Cleveland. She has the longest, blondest hair I ever saw. This is a picture of her. She's nice."

Once a week, once a month, or at whatever other interval works for you, slip the pictures into an envelope and mail them off to Grandma... or deliver them across town if she's a "nearby" grandma.

The same values and benefits that accrue from keeping A Journal for Grandma apply here.

It goes without saying that Grandma should, and will, preserve these pictures. Today, this year, with childish drawings underfoot, all over the tops of the bookcases and generally cluttering the house, you may not imagine finding those derrick-tall princesses and onion-turreted castles rare and precious. But if you don't hang on to your kids' artwork now, you'll find yourself missing it in twenty years. However, if you *didn't* hang on to it, Grandma will have... and you'll have that keepsake. Your kids, themselves, may even want to take over the collection in years to come as a record of their own childhoods.

Dear Family

*Materials needed: paper and pen, or typewriter,
or computer*

Another way of keeping in touch with family and preserving some of your family's history for posterity is to write letters. Depending on the size and closeness of your family, you may have only one relative to write to, or a dozen, and you may want to write an individual letter to each relative, write one letter addressed to all and make photocopies (or multiple copies from your computer), or send out one copy that follows a predetermined route, with Grandma and Grandpa sending it to Aunt

Jennifer, who sends it to Uncle Ed and Aunt Marti, who send it to...

With most families spread out across the continent, if not across the globe, most communication is at a distance. And even though Long Distance rates aren't as formidable as they once were, most of us are on enough of a budget that we can't afford to catch each family member up in detail on the week's happenings for our family, and every member of it.

But postage is still an affordable commodity.

There are various ways to make a "Dear Family" letter an all-family project. Everyone can sit at the dining room table, or around the computer in the den, or the typewriter in the living room, and put in their two cents' worth of input as to what should go into this week's letter:

"Tell about the frog I caught!"

"Don't forget my jarful of fireflies."

"Tell the family I'm going to my first dance Friday night."

"I got almost all **A**s on my report card. Don't forget to put that in the letter!"

Or everyone can write a few lines—or as many lines as they want—and all the pieces of paper can be clipped together and sent. (If you're one of the growing number of families in which someone works in a home office, you may have a photocopier at home with which to reproduce Billy's one-sentence report, Marilyn's one-pager, and Alisha's poem, along with your own letter.)

Sunday night is a good time to write the letter—it's a natural end to the week, a time when you can wrap up the week's events on paper for distant family members. But if Sunday nights are a bad time in your household, pick any other time that suits you. The important thing is just to write the "Dear Family" letter on a regular basis; *when* you write it is of little significance.

In years to come, if the letters have been saved, they'll provide a good record of the goings-on in your family from week to week. You can ask the last person in the chain—if it's distributed from family member to family member to family member—to return the letters to you for posterity when he or she is finished with them. Or that person may want to keep them. Just so *somebody* does.

I'll let my friend Vic Bobb tell you about *his* family's letters in his own words:

All the years I was growing up, my mother would sit down Sunday afternoons and pound out a long letter on her ancient Underwood. The letter was sent to her mother, who passed it among the three aunts, who passed it finally to my mother's sister. In those letters—this was back when a long distance phone call was a once-a-year, three-minute treat savored like Christmas or real maple syrup—Mom would catch her mom and aunts and sister up on all the things that had gone on during her hectic week as a young mother, wife, schoolteacher, housekeeper, seamstress....

Because the letters were directed to the four different sets of relatives through whose hands they would be passed, she always started the letters with the salutation, "Dear Fambly."

Fast-forward a couple of dozen years—not that the phrase "fast-forward" existed when the letters were being written. A Christmas during the Nixon administration, and the package from Bernell, my mother's sister, was grotesquely heavy. What in the world could the Smiths be sending? Rocks from the beach? Antique lead doorstops? Bowling balls flattened into packages the size and shape of four big cake pans?

In each package, it turned out, was a big brown leather album. On the front of each album, in gold stick-on letters, was the simple title, "DEAR FAMBLY."

And sure enough, that's what was in all those albums— two decades of letters, carefully and faithfully preserved by my aunt. In chronological order, with enclosures included (newspaper clippings about Cub Scout awards, drawings by the kids, all the interesting memorabilia that are some of the rivets holding together a family).

Nice as it is to reach out and touch someone, and handy and quick and wonderful as it is to keep in touch by phone, our lives today are not generating the kinds of physical record and accounting of our day-to-day lives that once upon a time helped preserve the past for the future.

If my grandfather had had the long distance habit in 1899, I wouldn't have the unspeakable treasure of the handwritten, elegantly phrased letter he wrote to his sister, telling all about meeting a young woman at church and finding himself "absolutely killed on her." The young woman came to be, within a year, my grandfather's wife...my father's mother.

Write a letter, if only every other week. Do continue to enjoy the pleasure of staying in touch with family by phone—but add the pleasure of writing, and bestow the pleasure of reading, on your family. Because of the letters I wrote to my parents during the nine years I lived in Illinois, I have a more thorough family record of the events and laughs and troubles of those years than I do of the glad-to-be-back-home decade I've spent back in the same area with my folks. It's nice to be here, to see them, to talk on the phone every couple of days...but I'm sure not creating the permanent and lasting record that letters used to create.

Write a letter. Write a lot of letters.

And keep copies of them. Maybe your recipients aren't as sensible as my Aunt Bernell.

Ancestral Halls

*Materials needed: one picture of each of your ancestors
for whom there's a picture available, plus one of you,
one of your spouse, and one of each of your kids; frames
or mats for each picture*

One of the simplest yet most effective and powerful ways for a
family to develop a strong sense of its identity, and of the
continuity from one generation to another, is by way of a family
portrait gallery. These pictures can be displayed in order (from
furthest-back ancestor to most recent family addition) along the
length of a hallway. The carefully selected pictures are apt to
show:

- A pair of stern-faced immigrants, circa 1880
- Their son at the time of his turn-of-the-century wedding
- His daughter as a young woman in Roaring Twenties dress
- Her son in his World War II uniform
- His daughter in sixties psychedelic outfit
- You, her daughter, in your wedding picture
- Pictures of your kids

The secret of a good family portrait gallery is to be judicious
in your choice of pictures. It's best if you choose just one picture
of each family member, and if that picture is of high
quality...not necessarily a formal studio portrait, but not that
picture just after you won the spaghetti-eating contest, with red
streaks all over your face, and not blurry, or Brownie-quality, or
"busy" photos, either.

If possible, have both sides of the family represented, and
both sides of each of these families, in turn. That is, assuming
you're not divorced, have pictures of both of your and your

spouse's parents, and if possible both parents of each of those parents, and so forth. But try to have each generation represented by at least one person.

If possible, frame or at least mat the pictures. The effect of photographs that have been prepared for display is much more dignified and impressive, and aesthetically pleasing, than a wall covered with taped-up snapshots, dorm-style.

You want the final effect to be both fun and dignified, somewhat formal and yet still alive. The result should make all the family members feel a part of a solid and meaningful entity. Portraits of ancestors can always be the impetus for the retelling of family stories. Was Grandma's portrait taking during her momentous visit to Chicago? Is Grandpa Albertson's photo the one that appeared in the paper when he helped found the first hospital in his county? Tell the kids the story behind the picture... or any story that the picture brings to mind about the relative shown in it.

And, as I've said elsewhere in this book, label the pictures on the back, so when questions arise in the future, you and the generations behind you will know who the people were, when the pictures were taken, and where. If you don't have all this information for every picture in the gallery, at least put all you do know on each picture.

Family Scrapbooks

Materials needed: blank scrapbooks, items to fill them with, possibly glue and paper for covers, pens

Blank scrapbooks are available in most any stationery store, discount store, and even some hobby stores. They're not expensive—your decision of whether to get one scrapbook for the whole family or one for each family member probably won't be based on price. You can even decide to do one scrapbook for the whole family *and* a scrapbook for each individual person.

You can get scrapbooks with mock leather covers, or decorative covers with designs or pictures on them, but you can also decorate your own...and isn't that more fun and more personalized?!

- You can cover the scrapbooks with construction paper, on which each child can draw his or her own preferred picture or design.
- Wallpaper makes a pretty and unique covering. Inquire at your neighborhood paint store for wallpaper samples or scraps they're discarding, or you may have wallpaper scraps left over from a job you've done in the house.
- The kids can decorate with cut-out comic strip characters pasted into a collage on construction paper, covered with plastic wrap.
- They can cut their initials or even whole names out of construction paper, or even out of gift wrap. (For economy, use leftover gift wrap from carefully unwrapped birthday presents.)

Of course you don't have to be limited by these suggestions if the kids have a different idea of how to go about covering their books—after all, they are *their* books. If it's a family scrapbook, chose a method or design you all agree on—perhaps your last name or initial cut out of paper and pasted on the front of a mock leather or other solid-colored scrapbook cover.

Now what goes *into* a scrapbook?

- For a family album, start with your wedding announcement. If you have only one copy of your announcement, and two or more kids want copies of it for *their* scrapbooks, use a photocopier and make copies.
- Include a copy of each child's birth announcement from the newspaper.

- If you live in a small town, and milestones in the kids' lives are written up in the paper, by all means include any such mentions. Was the entire nursery school graduating class mentioned by name? Did your kids' first communions, or bar mitzvahs, or bat mitzvahs get a notice in the paper? Clip all these and paste them in the scrapbook.
- Include ticket stubs from concerts or trips to the circus or the kids' first visit to a theatre to see a show, admission tickets if the family has been to a major theme park, and programs or directories from any of these places.
- Are the kids members of some rapper's, singer's, or actor's fan club? That may not seem important to you, but it's certainly big in their lives; if they got membership cards, let them put those in their scrapbooks.
- Also suitable for a scrapbook is any program from a school concert, play, or other production that one of your kids took part in. Does your child take dancing, singing, acting, or instrumental lessons? Does his or her school put on a yearly show or recital? Was a program handed out? Include it.

There may be something you haven't thought of that's important to your children. If they want to include their merit badges, now that they've dropped out of Scouts and no longer wear them, or a swimming certificate from summer camp—or virtually anything at all—remember, it's their scrapbook.

These are only guidelines. The choice of what's included should really be up to the child.

Virtually any type of memorabilia is suitable for a scrapbook. The only criterion that counts is, Is it important to the individual or the whole family that the scrapbook belongs to?

2

Brain- and Imagination-Stretchers

Invent a Game

Materials needed: varies

Once upon a time there was no Monopoly or Clue. Once upon a time there was no "A, my name is Alice," no stickball, no hopscotch, no tag, hide 'n' seek, or jump rope. *Somebody* invented every game that exists, whether generic or copyrighted.

While most of the copyrighted, boxed games were thought up by adults, most of the generics came from kids. You don't have to be a genius to think up a fun way to pass the time.

A game can be simple or complex. Set walnuts up on a fence, for example, and throw stones at them to knock them off. That's a pastime. Now make it a competition and devise a few rules to govern it. Say, for instance, that you've got to stand behind a tag line three feet away. For every walnut you knock over, you get a point. If you knock over all five walnuts with your first five stones, you win a bonus five points. The first player to reach thirty points wins. You've just invented a game!

Of course, not all games are competitive. There are cooperative games as well, though they're less common. And not all games involve two or more players; solitaire isn't the only solo game around.

Two things all games do have are *rules* and *an objective*. So if your family is going to invent a game, they need to keep that in mind. There are different types of games, including:

- Outdoor games
- Indoor games
- Active games
- Quiet games
- Board games
- Word games
- Other types

If your family has an interest in words, they may make up another Ghost or Hangman. If they're active, outdoors types, they may invent a new kind of relay race or other active game.

Your kids may have invented a game already and not even realize it. Did they ever take an existing game, change the rules so radically that it hardly seems the same, and possibly put a new name on it? Did they ever take a popular board game and use it with a whole new set of rules? They've invented a game.

But even if they've never gotten that creative before, they can start now. You can all put your heads together and see what you can dream up collectively, or you can all put your minds to the challenge individually and see what each can come up with.

There's an outside chance you'll put together something so stunningly marketable that you can sell the idea and see it produced commercially, but the odds against that are staggering. Really, your intent here should not be to get rich from your idea, but just to invent The _____ Family Game.

It could be a twist on an old game, or a combination of two games, or it could be a whole new concept. Whatever it is, you'll have extra pleasure when you all get together to play it, knowing you dreamed it up yourselves.

Now put those thinking caps on—and last one with a new game is a rotten egg!

*Bedtime Stories—
With a Twist*

*Materials needed: none, or possibly pen and paper or a
tape recorder to write down or record the stories*

There's no arguing the value of a bedtime story. In fact, I
should say *values*—plural—because bedtime stories provide so
much: The closeness between parent and child that snuggling
up for a story engenders, the settling-in routine that helps a
child unwind from the day's excitement and prepares him or her
for sleep, and the love of reading that's fostered by hearing Mom
or Dad read fascinating tales from a book each night.

With the three activities suggested here, kids still get the
first two benefits mentioned above, and for "love of reading"
substitute "stretching and exercising the child's own creativity."
These three types of bedtime stories can be substituted for a
traditional story read from a book, or you can set aside enough
time some evenings so that you can read a story to the kids from
a book *and* participate in one of the three types of bedtime
stories described below. In all of these, the child, or children,
spins out his or her own, individually created bedtime stories.

This, of course, helps develop a child's creativity and imagination, two areas that overdoses of TV can squelch the growth
of. In addition, the child will learn a little of the mechanics of
creating a story—the necessity for plot and good characters, the
building of suspense toward the resolution of conflict, the types
that exist both in fiction and in real life—conflict within
oneself, with other people, or with forces of nature and other

external circumstances. Who knows—you could be fostering
the budding of our next Mark Twain!

The child even has the opportunity to examine moral values
in the course of writing a story: Would it be right for the hero or
heroine to act in a particular way in a given circumstance? What
should the character do in this position? (What would your child
do in a similar circumstance?)

The child can be helped to think more clearly about the
consequences of people's actions, and about the feelings of other
people, if the parent stops to ask occasional questions: "How do
you think Bobby felt when the bad guy took his bike?" "Do you
think it was right for Chet to give Gary the answers to that test?
Why do you think it was wrong? What harm might it do?"

The stories can simply be told aloud without any attempt to
record them, or you, the parent, can write down the stories as
the kids spin them, or you can leave a small tape recorder
running, unobstrusively. (I'm not suggesting that you don't tell
the kids you're taping them, merely that you not make them
self-conscious by holding the recorder up to them as they
speak. Let it lie quietly nearby, with the mike aimed in their
direction.)

Basic Stories

The child is simply invited to invent a story. If you have more
than one child, each one can get a turn every evening (or every
evening that you engage in this activity), or each child can get a
turn on successive evenings.

If the child is absolutely stumped at inventing a character for
the story, you may choose to let him or her spin a yarn that
revolves around an existing character from a book, comic strip
or comic book, or TV show, but it's far better if he or she
stretches those "creativity muscles" by inventing a whole new
character instead of devising a new adventure for Winnie the
Pooh, the Ninja Turtles, Nancy Drew, or Mickey Mouse.

One way around the "I can't think of a character" problem is for the child to write a story about an existing real person—his best friend, her next-door neighbor, a teacher, or even the child himself or herself.

If the child has difficulty starting the story and can't think of a situation to put a character in, you can guide him or her along a creative path by posing a situation: "What do you think would happen if you woke up in the morning and found you'd turned blue with orange polka dots?" "What if a boy named Chris was walking down the street one day and found a talking dog?" "Suppose you invented a concoction with your chemistry set, and Mikey drank it while you weren't looking and suddenly became invisible?"

Before long, you should be able to stop providing prompting. The child's "creative muscles" will have been stretched by all your "suppose"s and "what-if"s, and she or he will be able to come up with situations (and characters to go with them) on his or her own.

Progressive Stories

With progressive bedtime stories, everyone chimes in, and each participating family member tells a part of the story in turn. This includes parents, too—in fact, till the kids get the hang of it, one parent may want to lead off the activity, starting the story and establishing the characters and situation.

Any number from two up can participate. The first person starts, tells a part of a story, and stops abruptly, leaving it to the next person to take over and carry on the story.

If the storyteller leaves Our Hero (or Heroine) in a predicament, so much the better, but not all stories will provide the opportunity for a cliff-hanger at every turn. Still, it's a challenge when Matt has the lead character trapped between an advancing pit bull and the edge of a cliff, and then he turns the story over to Susy and she has to get the hero out of his predicament. (Even Mom may be stumped at first, if it happens to be her turn when Matt breaks off the story with Our Hero in that quandary.

Or it may be Mom who does it to Matt, leaving him to come up with a solution that will help Our Hero escape that advancing alligator.)

As an alternative, you can make the progressive stories longer and let each person tell one installment per evening. Now, if Matt traps the story's hero in a seemingly unmanageable situation, Susy has twenty-four hours to think of how to get him out, before it's her turn to rescue the lead character and continue the story of his adventure.

Complete-the-Story

For this variation, you need a short book that the child has never read or heard before. This works best with picture books or short easy readers, as opposed to books with multiple chapters. The parent reads the story aloud to the child or children but stops a few pages before the end, at a point before the situation presented in the book is resolved.

Now the parent asks the child (or one of the children) to complete the story. (In a family with more than one child, it can be a different child's turn from one night to the next.) The child has to do his or her best to complete the story in a satisfactory way, resolving the conflict and tidying up the loose ends. After the child's version is complete, the parent reads aloud the rest of the book, giving the child a chance to see how the author of the book handled the resolution.

The parent should not present the author's resolution as the "right" one, merely as the "original" one. Children should not be made to feel that they are in a contest to see if they can come up with the "right" conclusion to the story, or the same one as the author. In fact, any story ending that works, is plausible, and ties up all the loose endings should be praised regardless of how close it is to the author's ending.

Fanta-Tease

Materials needed: none

Here's another imagination-stretcher that's good for any time you have from three to twenty minutes to occupy with your kids. Just pose a hypothetical question to them that stretches the limits of their everyday thinking and makes them look at things in creative ways. You can do this with one kid or five. A group of them may each try to outdo the others, coming up with responses to your questions that veer between sensible and outrageous.

Suggested questions to start you off:

- If space visitors landed in your yard, what would you show them?
- If you had four hands instead of two, what could you do that you can't do now?
- If you had eyes in the back of your head, what could you do that would be special or different?
- If you woke up tomorrow and found you were invisible, what would you do?
- If you had the traditional "three wishes" granted to you, what would you wish for?
- If you had five wishes granted to you, but with the condition that you couldn't wish for anything for yourself, what would you wish for?
- If you could invent an animal, what would you invent?
- If you had X-ray vision, what would you do with it?
- If you had the power to grant wishes, whose wishes would you want to make come true?
- If someone said, "Show me the three best things you know about in the world," what would you show him or her?

- If you could have any animal in the world for a pet, what would it be?
- If you could have any one super-power you wanted, what would it be and why?

Those questions should hold you and your kids through a few sessions of Fanta-Tease. After that, come up with your own questions. Then, for a change of pace, let the kids fire questions at you, and *you* come up with the answers. You'll still be stretching their imaginations.

If I Were _____

Materials needed: none

Got a space of time from a few minutes to an hour that you'd like to fill with something more constructive than sibling bickering or chatter about the latest rock star or movie idol? Something that's fun? Stretch the kids' imaginations and give them something to think about at the same time.

Pose a question like, "What would you do if you were President?" Get those brains geared up, and challenge the kids to some creative thinking. How would they improve the nation? The world? The quality of life for Mr. and Ms. Average Citizen? Who knows... you may indeed be harboring a future president, First Lady, or First Gent (what *will* we call the husband of our first female president?) among the junior members of your household.

Once you fully explore those possibilities, next time the kids have some spare "thinking time," stretch those imaginations in a different direction. Pose the following question: "What do you suppose life is like for a famous rap singer?" (Substitute "rock singer" or "movie star" if one of those is a category your kids can relate to better.)

They'll probably talk about money, glitter, fame, an entourage, and the other attractive trappings that go with such a life. Now ask them about privacy, the ability to just "hang out" with friends in a neighborhood restaurant without being bothered by adoring fans, and all the other hassles that comprise the down side of fame. Ask the kids provocative questions about the "other" side of being famous...and get them to consider the realities. Do they still envy their idols? Do they still think being rich and famous is everything?

More thought-provoking questions:

- "What would you do if you were head of a large corporation and one of your workers came up with an idea that would bring lots of money into the company but would seriously damage the earth's resources in the process?"
- "What would you do if you were head of a large corporation and one of the people under you came up with a great idea...but you found out he or she had gotten it by spying on one of your competitors?"

Now we're getting into some heavy questions that not only stretch the imagination but also challenge the kids to weigh moral and ethical issues. As they examine all sides of the questions, they may take stances that will serve them well not only later in life when they have to face ethical issues in business, but now, when they're tempted to cheat on a test or copy homework.

Another area of questions you may want to pursue:

- "If I were able to do three things for the Earth, I would _____."
- "What three things can you, as kids, do right now?"

This may lead to such projects as the kids volunteering to

help with recycling, picking up pieces of paper and other litter from sidewalks, or even planting a vegetable garden at home and growing organic, non-pesticide-tainted vegetables for the family. (See Earth-Friendly Families, page 79.)

You can use "If I Were _____ " questions purely to stretch the kids' imaginations, a worthwhile pursuit on its own, or you can involve them in examinations of ethics or questions of how to improve the world. ("If you were going to make the world a happier place for individual people, name three things you could do to brighten people's lives.") Whichever direction you take the questions in, you'll be stretching the kids' intellects and imaginations, making them think, and perhaps steering them toward some creative activities that really could make the world a nicer place to live in.

And while they're absorbed in contemplating the answers to the questions you've posed, they won't be staring goggle-eyed at the boob tube, blank-brained captives of the cathode-ray monster.

Critters

Materials needed: crayons, paper

Kids love to let their imaginations take off into the wild blue yonder, and it's good for them. But sometimes they need coaxing in the right direction. Here's a fun pastime for little-to-medium-sized kids: Invent strange critters, draw them, and give them names.

The animals your kids think up may be total inventions out of the blue, or they may be composed of different bits from animals that do exist in reality. Your kids may choose to cobble together the neck of a giraffe, the horn of a rhino, the tail of a pig, and various parts of other very real animals, winding up with a fabulous, fantastic critter that any zoo would vie to own.

It's better if they draw these animals in crayon, so they can depict them in color instead of black-and-white. Surely such outrageous creatures deserve to be drawn in hues that are as splendiferously absurd as the animals themselves!

As a further imagination-stretcher, you can ask your kids pertinent questions about their critters. If your son concocts a creature he calls a snairgabobble, ask him what sound a snairgabobble makes, what food a snairgabobble eats, where a snairgabobble lives, and any other pertinent questions that occur to you.

The imagination is a "muscle" that definitely should be exercised as often as possible.

Comical Books

Materials needed: 8½" × 11" paper (either typing paper or construction paper is fine), glue or paste, scissors, stapler, magazines and newspapers that you don't mind cutting up, pens or pencils

These aren't *comic* books—they're *comical* books. Home-made, they provide lots of laughs for kids both in the creation and in the enjoyment thereafter. And they're easy enough to make that any kid can do it.

Any number of pages is possible for one of these books, except that they are limited by the number of sheets your stapler will comfortably handle. If your household is one that has a heavy-duty stapler, and your kids are very creative and given to putting in lots of hours on a project, they can make one of these books out of more sheets of paper. But on average, five sheets is a good number per book. The stapler can handle the load, and the number of pages to fill won't tax your kids'—or your—creativity.

Start by neatly putting five sheets of ordinary $8\frac{1}{2}'' \times 11''$ paper—either construction paper or typing paper—together. Now fold them downward in half and turn them sideways, so you have surfaces $8\frac{1}{2}''$ high by $5\frac{1}{2}''$ wide to draw on. Fasten with two or three staples at the folded edge, as close to the edge as possible. If you've used five sheets of paper, you'll now have a twenty-page blank book to work with.

There are three ways to proceed from here. All involve writing a story on the left-hand pages only, with the right-hand pages holding the illustrations. The narrative on each left-hand page should be brief, perhaps one sentence per page, or two at most, so the complete stories are going to be short.

Variation 1

Each participant writes a short account of an adventure by some other family member—child or adult. This can be an actual experience or it can be purely fictitious, a realistic adventure or totally ludicrous.

Once the story is complete, the author searches through magazines and newspapers that the family has on hand, looking for pictures to illustrate the story—but she or he is not looking for pictures that *accurately* depict the actions, but pictures that are bizarrely comical in apposition to the text.

As an example, if the text says, "Then Kim got into her nicest dress to go meet the President," the picture selected might be of a woman coal miner in grungy, coal-blackened attire. Or of a woman in a muddy football uniform.

Another example: The text says, "Jackie was so pleased to see her handsome boyfriend, Dick, waiting for her on the front steps." The selected picture is of a lolling-tongued bulldog, or of one of the Three Stooges.

Variation 2

Each family member writes a story—true or fictitious—not about another family member but about himself or herself, then passes it to another family member, who does the illustrating.

Jack may have written about his heroics on the football field or his prowess in a bicycle marathon or his adventures as a grown-up firefighter, but when Colleen gets his book into her hands, the pictures she selects may tell quite a different tale!

Variation 3

Each participant selects the pictures first, gluing one in place on each right-hand page. He or she then passes the completely illustrated book to another family member, who now writes a story about one of the family members.

You can make it a rule that it has to be about the person who provided the illustrations, or you can allow the writer to choose any family member as his or her subject. But the story has to in some way—however bizarrely—tie in with the pictures.

When all the books are finished, pass them around in a circle, with everyone getting to read each book. Enjoy!

Illustrated Autobiographies

Materials needed: paper and pens (or typewriter or computer), pictures, paste or glue, blank books or binders or scrapbooks

The resemblance between this activity and Comical Books (see page 63) starts and stops with the fact that both involve illustrated stories of family members' lives. For where Comical Books may depict fictitious situations, these books are the honest-to-goodness true stories of the various family members. And where the illustrations of Comical Books are purposely at odds with the words, intended to provide comic relief, the pictures in Illustrated Autobiographies are legitimate illustrations of the various family members and the events in their lives.

You might think of them as photo albums with *lots and lots* of words, but actually the words are the most important thing here; if an event is important, and there are no pictures to illustrate it, it goes into the book anyhow.

And because these books are intended to endure, and to be added to frequently, something both more permanent and more flexible than the format of Comical Books is called for. There are any number of possibilities:

- A scrapbook or photo album can be used, with the typed or handwritten pages, and the pictures, being pasted into it till it's filled, at which point it's time to start Volume II.
- You can use a ring binder, typing on appropriate hole-punched paper (or on plain paper, leaving a margin wide enough for holes, and creating them yourself with a hole-punch).
- There are even books with blank pages and pretty covers

available commercially; this pretty well precludes typing or word-processing, but for handwriting and picture-pasting these work fine.

You may even come up with a solution that works better for you.

Each "author" writes his or her own autobiography. (Mom and Dad may have to help supply relevant details, such as the name of the hospital where Gloria was born, or just what year it was that Erik came down with chicken pox two days after his tonsils were removed.) It's up to each individual author just which events get included in his or her own book, and there are no "right" or "wrong" judgments here.

At the inception of this project, everyone can gather around the dining room table to write his or her book. This will probably lead to some fascinating "remember-when" sessions. If the recollections impede the work on the book, don't worry. Togetherness is a great thing, and the reminiscing can be just as satisfying an activity as the actual writing.

Stopping to rehash family picnics, Jerry's first ride on his bike without training wheels, or the time the bees chased Margery may take time away from producing the volumes of personal history. But if it takes two months longer to bring the books up to the present time in their accounts, it's not a problem. After all, no publisher is waiting; no deadline looms on the calendar.

Each child—and parent—should include those events that are meaningful, important, sad, funny, or otherwise memorable to him or her. Naturally some family members will produce thinner volumes than others, and not just because some kids have been on this earth less time than their siblings or parents have. Some are more detail-minded and will include virtually everything they remember; others will just hit the highlights. And everyone will have a different idea of what those highlights are.

You can raid the family photo albums for suitable pictures, or you can leave the albums alone, dig among the negatives, and reproduce a reasonable number of photos for the autobiographies. The kids may even choose to draw pictures to illustrate their stories, though photos are preferable for preserving family history as it happened.

At first, as I said, the family can work together, starting their books and bringing them up to the present moment. After that, family members may wish to work independently, each adding to his or her book as the occasion warrants. If you see that book production is lagging, though, there's no reason you can't from time to time declare a "book night" and have everyone gather at the dining room table to update their autobiographies.

It's a good idea if everyone starts work on the writing with a preconceived notion of which pictures are available to illustrate their books, and therefore which illustrations they'll have to leave room for. This is particularly true for those working longhand, especially in a prebound book where there's no latitude for inserting pictures after the fact. Working on a computer gives you more flexibility. Even working on a typewriter on loose-leaf pages gives you the ability to insert a page with a picture or two pasted to it.

These are not diaries. The authors should bear in mind that the family (and possibly others) will be reading them from time to time. This is not the place for older kids to detail crushes, loves, and other Deep Dark Secrets. These books are going to be read aloud (or possibly passed around the family circle, though reading aloud is a more companionable way to share them, one that involves the whole family at once).

As the project grows, each participant's excitement and success will spark higher levels of enthusiasm in the other family members, spurring them on to write more and more. If the family members are diligent in recording their autobiographies, in years to come they'll have a great way to look back and reminisce.

As the children grow to be adults, they'll appreciate their

parents' stories from an entirely new angle...especially many years from now, when their parents are no longer around. And the kids' own autobiographies will be preserved for *their* children to read in years to come. And maybe even their great-grandchildren.

Publishing houses won't start a bidding war over these books, and Hollywood isn't going to option them for star-studded spectacles, but they'll be altogether satisfying to write, to re-read, to share with other family members...and to share with future generations.

Write an Illustrated Book

Materials needed: paper, pen, possibly typewriter or computer, crayons or watercolors or markers. (Optional: construction paper, scissors, paste or glue)

Here's another project that can use the multiple talents of your family. The primary aspect of this one is writing a book— actually a short story will do. If you have more than one child, they can collaborate on writing the story together, or one can write it and the talents of the other(s) can be utilized in other ways.

One person can illustrate the book, probably using either crayons, watercolors, or markers. And if you have a typist, or someone with extremely pretty handwriting, in the family, that person can either type the book up or neatly write the story.

The illustrations can go on separate pages, or the person writing or typing the book can leave room on certain pages, at the illustrator's direction, for pictures to be drawn right onto those pages. Someone can make a pretty cover, too, possibly out of construction paper. The title can be drawn on the paper, or you can cut, out of contrasting-colored construction paper, the letters that comprise the title.

Occupied by Design

Materials needed: pen or pencil and paper

What kid doesn't like drawing? What kid doesn't like designing things? Prod your child's imagination to grow while keeping him or her occupied in a creative excercise. Next time your child is bored, put a pen or pencil and some sheets of scrap paper in front of him or her, and ask him or her to design something... something in particular. There are plenty of possibilities.

Many girls, of course, get into designing clothing, or doll's clothing, without any prodding from their parents, but boys, too, can design clothing. The lead-in to a clothing-design session might be a discussion of different styles of clothing around the world. Open your dictionary or, even better, your encylopedia if you have one, and examine kilts, dirndls, suits of armor, and various other garments worn in different parts of the world and over the various centuries.

Ask your child—male or female—to design the most comfortable and practical clothing he or she thinks a man or woman might wear. Or ask him or her to design a possible outfit to be worn by a man or woman in the twenty-first century... or the twenty-second.

How about a practical, if fashion-defiant, outfit for right now? Call it Useful Clothing. A pair of pants might feature one or more of the following:

- A pocket that contains a tiny, folding, lightweight vinyl raincoat (to be included with the outfit), very useful in case of sudden rain.
- A tripod with flat top that telescopes out from the seat of the pants, to be sat on while waiting at the bus stop, on line for movie tickets, or in other waiting situations.
- A strap attached to the waistband for carrying schoolbooks home.

Another design challenge you can throw in your child's direction is to invent a product that will help make life easier for people. Or to invent a product that will make life more fun. Yet another challenge: Invent a new game. Or design a new toy.

Moving away from inventions but still within the realm of designing: Ask your child to draw a floor plan for his or her' room that is rearranged to be in some way better than the present layout. You can, if you wish, allow the child to incorporate new furniture, or you can make it a requirement that he or she utilize only existing furniture, shelves, etc. (This will depend in part on whether you have any intention of actually carrying out the plan, or if it's just an exercise in the wild blue yonder.)

The next natural step may be to ask him or her to design a piece of furniture—for any room in the house—that would be both practical and attractive.

Since this is not a competitive activity, it's one that naturally lends itself to both one-child and multichild families. An "only" child can sit down and draw, with input from Mom or Dad when needed, as easily as four siblings can sit and draw either together or independently. The whole family—parents included—can get in on the designing as a unit, with each person having input. This is a good exercise in cooperation, getting the kids used to working with others on a project, respecting others' ideas, and even learning how to gracefully deflect ideas that don't work without attacking their inventor.

If your child really gets into designing, there's no limit to the number of things he or she can plot out. How about:

- A plan for twenty square blocks of a new city?
- A 2010 model car?
- A luxury yacht?

You may have a future architect, engineer, city planner, clothing designer, or inventor in your household. And even if your child's future lies in a different direction, you're exercising his or her imagination and creativity...a worthwhile pursuit regardless of the future.

Design Outrageous Hats

Materials needed: pen or pencil and paper

This sounds like a project for girls, but actually boys and men wear caps or hats as well, and we're not talking about *pretty* hats here; we're talking silly...and possibly functional.

Girls may want to design chapeaus with ridiculous quantities of flowers, veils, and gewgaws on them, but both boys and girls—and Moms and Dads, because there's no reason for parents not to get in on the act—may want to design other types of hats as well:

- Fishing hats with containers dangling from them in which to carry the bait

- Golf hats with built-in suspended sunglasses
- Broad-brimmed hats with many pockets built around the crown, for carrying things that won't fit in your clothing's pockets
- Beach hats with straps to hold suntan lotion, and pockets to hold money and keys, so you can wear your swimsuits to the beach and never worry about not having clothes on in which to carry necessities

Those are just some suggestions. What can your kids come up with?

Powers of Observation

Materials needed: none, or possibly pens and paper

How good are your child's powers of observation? Test them out, and make him or her more aware of his or her surroundings. Without warning, tell your child to close his or her eyes— or possibly you could cover your child's eyes with your hands or a blindfold. Now ask the child to describe the most familiar objects, preferably ones that are going to be within sight when he or she opens his or her eyes. Depending where you are at the time, these might include the exterior of your house, your living room, even you yourself. In lieu of selecting objects immediately within sight, you can choose something nearby that the two of you can go to, to check on your child's accuracy, as soon as he or she is done describing them.

See how accurately, and in how much detail, your child describes these familiar objects. See if she or he pays attention to such items as colors, shapes, sizes, and little details, such as:

- How many windows there are on the second floor on the front of the house?
- Whether the front porch has latticework on it?
- How deep the pile is on the living room carpet?
- Whether the clothing you currently have on has pockets in it?
- Whether all the windows in the room are fully open, some are partially open, all are closed, or some combination?

Did he or she notice such information as:

- If the plant on the window sill is droopy from lack of water.
- If there are cassette tapes lying next to the stereo.
- If there's a book lying open on the end table.
- If sunlight is streaming in the east window.

Testing your child's powers of observation is more than a fun pastime; it's a reminder to him or her to walk with eyes open, to not look past things but to actively look *at* them, to *see* them.

If you have more than one child (and assuming they're old enough to write), you can even turn this exercise into a contest. Sit your kids down at the dining room or kitchen table—in some place other than the area you want them to describe. Give them each a pen and paper and time them, giving them five minutes to describe everything about another room of the house, or the exterior of it. Choose a common area, such as living room, dining room, kitchen, family room, finished attic or basement, or exterior, not one of their bedrooms, which one would be more familiar with than the other, unless you have only two kids and both share a room. See, at the end of the five minutes, which of your kids has described the most details the most accurately. (Also see Eyewitness, page 93.)

Powers of Description

Materials needed: none, or possibly pens and paper

How facile with words are your kids? How easily can they describe objects, people, feelings, seasons, anything at all? The ability to express oneself is important to everyone at some time, if only to avoid being misunderstood. In business, expressing oneself with clarity is a must. Writers need to express themselves descriptively, with a few well-chosen words that paint a picture the reader can see in his or her mind's eye. Witnesses to a crime need to describe the suspect adequately and accurately to the police. Lovers need to describe their feelings to each other. People building a house need to explain themselves succinctly to the architect on the job to be sure of getting what they want. No matter what you're doing in life, being able to describe things well is important. And it's never too early to start.

So sit your kids down and get each one to describe familiar objects. These can be either things they're very familiar with, or things they have right in front of them. In some cases, a brief sentence will be all that's feasible; in other cases, a paragraph or two may evolve. At very least you're looking for accuracy and clarity, though a poetic description is wonderful if the child has a talent for writing.

Suggested items to have them describe could include:

- A particularly striking, impressive tree in your yard
- Trees in spring
- The full moon
- Your family pet
- A baby (either *any* baby or a particular baby)

- A model ship or car that you might have around the house
- Your family car
- Freight trains in general
- Their school building
- A local park you visit often
- Their grandparents.

But don't restrict yourself to those topics. Pick other subjects the kids might be familiar with and interested in. If you want, you can give them pens and paper and let them write their descriptions, but it's not necessary, unless you're having them compete against each other for most accurate or poetic descriptions, and you want each to write without the others knowing what he or she is saying.

Get them to hone those powers of description. They'll serve them well later in life.

3

Practical Projects

Earth-Friendly Families

Materials needed: paper, pen or pencil, crayons

Is yours a family that's Earth-friendly? Do you conserve energy, recycle, and follow the other precepts of making this a "green" planet? Even if you're not heavily involved in the movement, there are plenty of things you and your family can do to make this old Earth a little healthier.

Maybe you already do some of these things, taking them for granted:

- Using cloth diapers rather than disposable
- Washing dishes by hand rather than in the machine
- At least waiting till you have a full machine before running the washer

But do your kids know why you do these things? Are they Earth-aware?

A good place to start is with a discussion. If they don't know about pollution, depletion of the Earth's resources, thinning of the ozone layer, and all the other problems that plague our planet, start by explaining them in terms appropriate to the ages of your kids.

Now have them make two lists, one of Earth-friendly activities, the other of Earth-unfriendly ones. If they can't think of any at first, give them a few hints, or start the list off yourself with a few examples. When the lists are made, discuss the various items on them with the kids. How many activities on each list is *your* family doing? What can you do about seeing to it that you do more of the "friendly" activities and fewer of the "unfriendly" ones?

In case you, too, are stuck trying to think of items to put on each list, some Earth-friendly activities include:

- Bringing canvas bags to the store so you don't have to bring home groceries in paper or plastic
- If you don't have canvas bags, bringing the store's paper or plastic bags back with you on your next shopping trip for re-use
- Recycling
- Bicycling
- Picking up litter wherever you encounter it
- Conserving water
- Using fewer disposables such as diapers, paper plates, and plastic utensils
- Doing dishes by hand
- If using the dishwasher, waiting till you have a full load
- Ditto for the clothes-washer if yours doesn't have a water level setting
- Planting flowers and trees
- Growing your own vegetables
- Turning off lights when you leave a room that no one else is in, if you don't expect to return within five minutes

Some Earth-unfriendly activities include:

- Driving
- Leaving unnecessary lights burning
- Letting water run from a faucet when not immediately in use
- Taking long showers/tall baths
- Letting a helium balloon go up into the sky (because when it deflates it will come back to Earth, where at the very least it will be litter, and at worst some animal could

swallow it and die or choke on it while trying to swallow it)
- Spraying anything out of an aerosol can that contains CFCs (chlorofluorocarbons)
- Holding the fridge door open longer than is needed to put food away or take it out
- Chopping down trees

After you and your kids have made these two lists, make another one: Ten Specific Ways We Can Help the Earth. On this list, you and your kids can make specific, practical suggestions for ways your own family can help make the Earth healthier. (If your kid says, "I can skip baths," decline with the offer, "No, but you can take baths in a lower level of water.")

You can also help promote their Earth-awareness by having them draw pictures or even write stories about recycling and other Earth-friendly activities.

Then follow up on it. Make sure they stick to their part of the bargain, doing the things they said they'd do and avoiding the Earth-unfriendly behaviors they said they'd avoid.

You do your part, too.

Keepsake Box

*Materials needed: box. Possible optional coverings or
decoration for it include any of the following: glitter;
inexpensive imitation jewels; construction paper, with
either crayons, paints, or markers to decorate it; cut-out
photos, sports pictures, or comic character pictures, to
make a collage; yarn; wallpaper; gift wrap; shells; and
glue*

Elsewhere in this book I've discussed scrapbooks. But what
of the keepsakes that don't fit in a scrapbook yet deserve saving
and treasuring? By whatever name, a keepsake box, treasure
box, or memento box keeps your child's treasures safely and
neatly stored away for future enjoyment and remembering.
Every child can have one; it's easy. The family can also have one
for family keepsakes.

The size of the box will depend on how many treasures the
child or family has and what size they are, and also on what size
sturdy box is available. Something along the lines of a cigar box
is sturdier than a flimsier cardboard box; a local store may be
able to provide something even larger and more resilient.

We are not talking about a toy chest here, though some toys
and paraphernalia could qualify as treasures. Does your son
have as a keepsake the ball with which he hit his first sandlot or
backyard home run? That certainly goes in the treasure box!
Does your child have a cartoon character watch he or she has
outgrown and will no longer wear, yet secretly treasures? Put it
in the box! A small autograph book passed around the bunk at
the end of summer at camp? There's another candidate for the
box!

In fact, virtually any keepsake that's not flat and small enough for a scrapbook is suited for a treasure box. Is the family saving a map marked from a trip you all took together? A program from a day at the ballpark that's too thick to fit comfortably in a scrapbook? Into the treasure box it goes!

Decoration is optional. Some kids don't give a hoot about what the box looks like, only about its contents. Fine—they can leave it plain. Perhaps they'll want to decorate it next year. (perhaps not). Other kids will care almost as passionately about the box as about its contents.

- They can use sprinkles and glue, decorating in a random pattern, or draw their names, initials, or just a picture in glue, then cover the glue with sprinkles.
- The child can glue a piece of colorful yarn down to form her or his name or initials.
- Girls may like to glue on large, colorful, inexpensive imitation "jewels."
- Girls or boys can glue on shells. (In fact, shells from a special trip or rocks with a particular significance or just great beauty may be among the contents of the box.)

Some of the same suggestions for covering a scrapbook (see page 47) work for treasure boxes too:

- Construction paper can be pasted to the box after it's been drawn or painted on, or after the child has pasted on it a collage of sports pictures from a magazine, comic strip characters, or photos of the child at various ages, among other possibilities.
- Again, as with the scrapbook, wallpaper works as a covering, or gift wrap, though gift wrap may be too flimsy to endure over the years.

But don't worry—as your children's treasures grow in number, they're likely to need a larger box every few years, unless they're the type who systematically weed out old stuff and get rid of it as they acquire newer treasures. If a newer-larger box is necessary every few years anyhow, it's less crucial if the decorations on the old box are beginning to wear or fray.

If some of your son's or daughter's keepsakes look question-able in significance to you, remember it's not just the *object* being saved—it's the memories that object evokes. That pressed dandelion may be one of the "flowers" your daughter's class-mates gave her when she starred in the first-grade play. That ugly, nondescript rock in your son's treasure box may be one he threw at an impossibly distant target...successfully...to win the admiration of a group of older kids. Unless space or hygienic considerations are relevant, allow your kids to be the judge of what's a suitable keepsake for their individual boxes, even if you have more say in what goes into the family treasure box.

How Does Your Garden Grow?

Materials needed: seeds, gardening implements

If you have a yard of any semireasonable size, why not turn at least part of it into a family garden? You can have one large whole-family garden (at least, as large as space and time to work on the garden permit), or each family member can have his or her own small plot.

A family garden is a rewarding project on many levels. First of all, it teaches responsibility. (If any family member fails to keep up his or her share of the responsibility, the garden is going to suffer. If watering, weeding, and other chores such as transplanting seedlings aren't accomplished—and on time—

the unfortunate and possibly even disastrous results will be visible.)

But on the other hand, if family members are diligent in their work on the garden, the results will be both satisfying and gratifying. The results of the effort will be visible in the daily progress of the vegetables (or flowers, or both) as they grow and grow in the garden.

And children who are reluctant to eat their veggies will be a lot more willing if they grew the carrots or string beans themselves.

Assigning a plot to each child is generally a better idea than assigning a task to each child within a whole-family garden. But it can be done that way, giving each child a day to water, a day to weed, etc., with appropriate adult supervision where called for. Adult supervision is especially desirable in matters like pruning, transplanting seedlings, and other tasks where knowledge or judgment are more relevant than simply in watering. (Even weeding may require some supervision at first, otherwise struggling young veggies may mistakenly be plucked as weeds.)

If all the kids (and parents) share the tasks in a common garden, there's a diminished sense of pride in performance. And when a mishap strikes, and part of the crop fails, finger-pointing is inevitable: "It's your fault—you forgot to water them!" "Did not! I watered them when I was supposed to. It's gotta be *your* fault!"

So it's generally better to let each child have his or her own plot... and no one but himself or herself to blame if proper care isn't taken. Of course, if it rains too much, predatory animals eat the foliage, or some other natural disaster strikes, that's unfortunate... but the fact that sometimes we fail despite our best efforts is a lesson in life the kids have to learn sooner or later.

On the other hand, you need to be reasonable in just how large a plot you expect a child to take care of, and how much help you give him or her. Depending on the child's age, he or she may need parental help digging before planting, or even reading the instructions on the seed packet. A few reminders at the beginning to water and weed are also necessary in most cases.

The choice of crops should be made by both you and the kids. Let them have some input into which crops they're going to grow, but do guide them away from those that involve more work than they're realistically going to be able to do, that are too difficult to grow successfully, or that aren't suited for your climate or soil conditions. Read the seed packet, read the catalog if you're mail-ordering, or ask for guidance at the store if you're purchasing in person.

Giant sunflowers grow quickly (good for kids impatient to see the results of their labors) and provide seeds that are delicious and nutritious. They're also spectacular to look at. Radishes and tomatoes are another good choice. These vegetables grow fairly easily, and the kids will enjoy snacking on the results of their labors.

And then, if the kids are old enough to handle a knife respectfully, you can teach them to make rosettes from the harvested radishes. Kids love to "cook decoratively" and will enjoy making salads they can garnish with a radish rosette at the center of the top of the salad.

The whole family can work on the garden simultaneously, each on his or her own patch, though if such togetherness doesn't work into your family's schedule, there's certainly no reason for each family member not to work on his or her little plot at the time that suits him or her best. Such solo sessions help foster the child's ability to work without supervision, and to persist even when the reward for work is not immediately evident.

If you live in an apartment, you can select plants, flowers, and even vegetables that can be grown in window boxes... depending in part on your climate, and on how much sunlight your windows get. Inquire in your local garden-supply store or plant store.

Pizza to Stay

Materials needed: one 10″ × 12″ cookie sheet with edges.

For the crust: 4 cups flour, 1 to 1¹/₂ cups water, two packages (or about 5 tsp) yeast, 1/8 tsp salt, 1 Tbs granulated sugar, 3 Tbs olive oil (you can substitute vegetable oil but it won't taste as authentic). Optional: A dash of warm beer

For the sauce: 15-oz. can of tomato sauce, 1/2 tsp garlic powder or more to taste, 1 Tbs olive oil, a sprinkle of oregano or Italian seasoning, (Optional: small can of tomato paste)

Toppings: 1 Tbsp (or more to taste) of oregano, or Italian seasoning, 1¹/₂ lbs mozzarella cheese (you can substitute Monterey Jack, which is more flavorful, but it's less authentic), and any or all of the following: one large sliced onion, 6-8 oz. pepperoni, 12-16 oz. ground Italian sausage, green pepper, olives, fresh or canned mushrooms, anchovies

"Hey, Mom, what's for dinner?"

"Pizza."

"Yay!"

The response is always enthusiastic when "Pizza" is the answer, but think how much more enjoyable the pizza will be when the kids have a chance to make it themselves! (Think how much more affordable it'll be, too.) Making a pizza from scratch at home gives everyone in the family the chance to have theirs perfectly customized, too, with no extra charge for extra toppings.

The precise ingredients will depend on the tastes of your

family, but the recipe provided here will serve as the ideal foundation, on which you can ring any number of changes. Depending on the ages of the kids in your family, even gathering the ingredients can be part of the project. Young kids enjoy helping with marketing, especially when they know the end result is going to be pizza, and not only that, but a pizza they're going to bake themselves.

How you divide up the cooking chores, once you get the ingredients home, will, of course, depend on the number and ages of kids in your household, and how respectful they are of kitchen tools such as knives. But here are the basic instructions:

The crust, from homemade dough, is so tasty it may spoil you so you'll never again enjoy a commercial pizza. Put the two packets of yeast in a large mixing bowl, add about a tablespoon of granulated sugar, then pour in one cup of quite warm (but not hot) water. Stir with a fork till the yeast is dissolved, then set it aside in a warm place to get the yeast into a growing frenzy.

While the yeast is doing its thing, slice the onion, slice the cheese into generous but not too fat slabs, slice the peperoni, if using, into thin circles, and prepare whatever other topping ingredients, such as mushrooms, green peppers, or anchovies, your family wants.

Fry the sausage if this is one of your toppings.

When the yeast mixture has begun to foam or bubble, make your dough: Start adding the flour to the yeast mixture, a little at a time, stirring it with a fork, till there's enough flour in the mixture so that it has ceased to be a liquid. Add half a teaspoon of salt, and, if desired for your taste, a little more sugar. As it stiffens beyond the capacity of a fork to mix, add the rest of the flour gradually and work it into a mass with your hands. Kneading the dough may be so enjoyable to the kids that you'll have to call "Time" on each participant to give the next child a turn.

Once the dough is kneaded, add three tablespoons of olive oil and knead it some more, till the oil is wholly integrated into the dough. If things have gotten a little too sticky, bring the consistency back to correctness with a little more flour. Precise measurement of flour and water is not that important in this recipe, so don't sweat it if you think you're a little off. You haven't wrecked the dinner.

For a lighter, higher-rising dough, add a foamy dash of warm beer, then add enough flour to bring it back to the proper consistency. The dough will eventually be a mass of considerable size; be sure that it has been thoroughly kneaded, then cover it and put it into a warm place to rise.

If you haven't sliced all the veggies, or the sausage hasn't all been fried yet, now's the time to do it. Now is also the time to make the sauce: Pour a can of tomato sauce into a bowl and add a tablespoon of olive oil. If thicker, more intense sauce is more to your liking, add a small can of tomato paste. Season the sauce with either garlic powder or fresh-squeezed garlic juice, onion powder if desired, and a couple of pinches of oregano (or Italian Seasoning).

By now the dough should have risen. You can punch it down and allow it a second rising; if your family is impatient, though, that isn't crucial. Roll or knead the dough out flat. You'll almost certainly have more than necessary to cover a 10″ × 12″ oblong cookie sheet; we'll deal with the leftover dough in a minute. Meanwhile, this word: You're making a thick-crust pizza, so don't strive for the paper thinness you sometimes get in commercial pizza. A crust in the ¼″ to ⅜″ range is fine.

Right about now is a good time to preheat your oven to 450°F.

Pour a little puddle of olive oil in the center of the cookie sheet and rub it all over the surface and up the edges, to grease it well. Sprinkle a bit of flour onto the flat surface, and tip the sheet this way and that till the whole surface is pale.

Drape the big flattened glob of dough over the cookie sheet, then flatten and mold the dough to the sheet, smooshing the surface fairly flat and building protective crust walls all the way around. Here's where the extra dough gets removed and reserved for later use.

Pour another dab of olive oil onto the surface of the dough, spreading it with your hand till the whole surface, including the up-sloping sides, glistens. If your family's tastes run to heavy garlic, sprinkle garlic powder over the olive oil; otherwise, skip that step. Now stir the sauce that's in the bowl a little bit and pour it onto the pizza. Spread it around, sprinkle it with garlic powder to taste, and shake on oregano (or Italian Seasoning).

Spread your loose-cooked Italian sausage, if using, by hand. Grab a handful of the meat and spread it out over the pizza. (You cooked it ahead of time so it will have cooled down by the time you're ready to handle it.) To be healthful, make every attempt to squeeze the grease out of it or drain the grease off beforehand. But for extra flavor, you can drizzle a little of the grease into the sauce if you want.

Now cover the surface of the pizza with the sliced peperoni and whatever other toppings you've elected to use. Once everything is in place, cover the whole affair with your cheese slabs. It's ready to go into the oven, which should be up to 450° by now.

Meanwhile, you have leftover crust. You have two options regarding this. One is to form it into little loaves about the size of your fist and bake them the next morning to provide personal-sized hot bread for breakfast.

Your other option is to let your kids make little personal pizzas out of the extra dough. Do your kids hate sausages but love mushrooms? Hate pepperoni but love green peppers? Are you adults anchovy-lovers, to the kids' chagrin? They can fix up their personal pizzas exactly to their satisfaction.

Start peeking at the big pizza about eight minutes after you put it in, though it's more likely to take ten to twelve minutes. You'll know it's done when the cheese is melted and bubbling, though the best clue of all is to peek at the underside of the crust—when it's gotten golden, you've got your ready-to-devour pizza. (If you've made personal pizzas with the leftover dough, they won't take as long, so keep a sharp eye out for them.)

As for the big pizza, when you remove it, cut it into big, gloppy, drippy squares, pass out forks to all who are concerned about manners or messy hands, and dig in. You can feed five or six gluttons from the recipe.

Warning: This isn't a project you want to undertake every other night if you're health-conscious or weight-conscious—it *is* high in cholesterol, salt, and fat...and you'd better lay in a supply of juice, or milk, or soda, as it'll probably make everyone thirsty. But the taste is great, so's the fun, and so's the togetherness in making it.

Compile a Recipe Booklet

Materials needed: paper and pen, possibly typewriter or computer

As discussed in several places elsewhere in this book, kids like to cook. Why not take whatever recipes you have, or know by heart, that are suitable for kids and compile them in a booklet, "The _____ Family Recipe Book"? Include your kids' favorites as well as any others you can think of that they may not have tried yet but could handle—possibly with a little parental help.

Obviously a four-year-old, an eight-year-old, and a twelve-year-old are at different levels of cooking ability—as well as the ability to handle sharp knives and other kitchen implements safely. But you can even compile the booklet with a view to the future, thinking of recipes your eight-year-old might be ready for in two years.

Explain the procedures in clear, simple, yet detailed words.

A child may not know precisely what "whip" means, as in "whip the cream," or "fold," as in "fold the egg whites into the batter." Explain the procedures in as much detail as you feel is necessary, so the kids know what's expected of them.

Instead of using abbreviations like "T" for tablespoon, you may want to spell the measurements out. Or, to get the kids ready for grown-up cookbooks that do have standard abbreviations, you may want to use them, too, but include a glossary at the front of the book that translates "T" or "tsp" or "cu" into fully spelled-out words.

You can write these recipes down yourself, or one of the kids can take them down. A parent or older sibling who know how to may want to neatly type them so you can make a more professional-looking (and more enduring) booklet than a hand-written one would be.

And if the kids are enterprising types, they'll get quadruple the pleasure out of the book. First, they'll enjoy helping write the book. Second, they'll enjoy using it, cooking the foods the recipes are for. Third, they'll enjoy eating what they've cooked (even veggies taste good when you've made them yourself). And finally, they can duplicate the book, if you've typed it on computer or if you have a photocopier in your home, as many people do these days. Then they can set up a "lemonade stand" outside the house—only instead of lemonade, they'll be selling recipe books!

Eyewitness

Materials needed: VCR, TV, tape of a segment of a movie or TV show involving some action, pens, and paper

Suppose you were to witness a crime being committed? How helpful would you be when the police came around asking questions? Just how observant *are* you, anyhow?

These are the questions for which the game of Eyewitness provides answers... about all the people playing, which in this case is going to be you and the members of your family.

For maximum effect, it's best if no one but the person who sets up the game knows in advance that questions are going to be asked after the video/movie clip is shown. If need be, though, you can let the family in on what's happening.

Choose a clip just a few minutes long, involving some sort of action—I don't mean it has to be violent action, just action. If at all possible, the clip should be from a movie or show with which no one is already familiar. Have the taped show or movie set up in the VCR, ready to roll at the point at which the scene in question starts. Gather your family around the TV set, ask them to watch, and start the VCR going.

At the end of the scene, pass out paper and pens, asking everyone to write down exactly what they've just seen, in their best eyewitness fashion. Ask each person to provide his or her own account of what went on in the scene, including not merely the sequence of action but also whatever details they may have noticed. When everyone's done writing, have each person take a turn at reading his or her notes aloud.

What will prove interesting, as family members read their eyewitness descriptions aloud, is the extent to which versions will vary. The family will discover that, even immediately after an incident, different people experience different things even in the same situation. People pick up on different details. Some will be more aware of the physical action, some of the clothing worn by the participants, or the cars, if any, or the animals present, if any, or the general surroundings in which the scene takes place. Variances in the accounts of even the core action are likely.

As family members read aloud, others should feel free to speak up and express disagreement:

"The guy behind the desk had a moustache."

"No, he didn't!"

They'll express amazement:

"Did anyone notice what the woman in the truck was wearing?"

"That was a *woman?!*"

They'll be surprised at themselves:

"I didn't even notice there were two dogs next to the fat man."

If desired, you can act as a questioner, asking such questions as,

"Can anyone tell me what the dentist's hair looked like?"

"Did anyone else notice the thin man behind the man behind the desk?"

The results of this activity will almost certainly be enlightening and surprising. Family members will be amazed at how many details they missed. They'll be amazed at how different accounts of the same scene will vary from each other, almost as if, in some cases, people were watching two different movie clips.

You'll learn something about yourselves and each other, in the light of which items were most noticed by each person. You'll each feel, by turns, smug at how you got some details that no one else did, and chagrined that you missed some perhaps significant details that the others caught.

Hopefully, this exercise will make your family conscious of the extent to which we miss details of real-life scenes we witness or are involved in. It will prod everyone to be a more conscious observer of life as it happens around them. It will make them more willing to accept others' accounts of scenes, less quick to call someone a liar because the other person's recollection of an event differs from theirs.

If you repeat the game, it can help your family develop their powers of observation and the habit of using those powers. The goal, of course, is not to become ideal crime scene witnesses; it is to become people who are truly involved in the world around them.

If you conduct this activity a second time, family members will be aware of what's coming and will be more intent on memorizing the scene so they can report more complete and accurate details. But even knowing they're going to be quizzed, not everyone will remember everything, or remember accurately that which they do report. Even under these circumstances, the members of your family will learn a lot about themselves and each other as a result of what they notice and remember.

And it will be fun.

4

Holiday Happenings

Thanksgiving Wreath

Materials needed: one twelve-inch cane or wicker wreath; one can of gold spray paint; glue; two cups assorted nuts, such as almonds, filberts, pecans, still in their shells; one small bunch of dried flowers; old newspaper

Spray the nuts and dried flowers thoroughly with the gold spray paint and set aside on the newspaper to dry. When they have dried, arrange them artfully on the wreath, till you are satisfied with the placement. Then glue them all in place.

Start a New Tradition— Thanksgiving Caroling

Materials needed: none

Of course we've all heard of Christmas carolers. They go from door to door, singing Christmas songs and bringing good cheer to the families they visit. It's a charming tradition, one that brings a smile to the face of virtually all but the hardest-hearted Scrooge among us.

But why should singing holiday songs from door to door be confined to Christmas? There are several good Thanksgiving songs; have you ever thought of going around your neighborhood singing them—as a family? Wouldn't your neighbors love to hear the harmoniously blended voices of your family raised in "Come, Ye Thankful People Come," or "We Gather Together"?

Be daring…start a *new* tradition, one your family can lay claim to as *yours*, one *you* originated…at least in your neighborhood. Go out and sing, and bring good cheer to your neighbors while engaging in an activity that involves the whole family in an activity that's harmonious both literally and figuratively.

And if Thanksgiving caroling catches on in your neighborhood, think of all the good songs there are to sing on Memorial Day or the Fourth of July: "America the Beautiful," "America," "The Star Spangled Banner," "The Battle Hymn of the Republic," "God Bless America," and others.

Miniature "Christmas Trees"

Materials needed: large pine cone, jar lid that is just slightly bigger than the base of the pine cone, small sheet of aluminum foil, glue, paint or tinsel or glitter or sequins

At the Christmas season, when the kids are impatient for the big day (and the big haul of presents they expect!), one way to assuage their impatience is to give them a holiday-flavored project to get involved in. These festive Christmas decorations cost next to nothing to make and are ridiculously easy, too.

Start with the lid from a jar. After making sure it's clean, cover it with aluminum foil, then glue the base of the pine cone to the foil-covered lid. Decorate the cone by painting it or draping small bits of tinsel on it, or you can sparingly glue on glitter to give it sparkle. Another possibility is to glue on a small number of red and green sequins.

That's all there is to it, and you now have a holiday decoration that can sit on the floor at the base of the tree before you pile the presents around the tree, or that you can put on shelves or other surfaces to dress up the house with Christmas cheer.

Candy Cane Container

Materials needed: large empty can, box of candy canes whose length equals or exceeds the depth of the can, glue, ribbon approximately twelve inches long. (Optional: green crepe paper, scissors)

This inexpensive project can involve the whole family at once, each working on his or her own container. You can place the containers around the house, during the holiday season, using them simply as decorations or as containers for pencils, sprigs of evergreen, the kids' small toys such as marbles or jacks, or any other little items. You can even place a small single flower from the florist's in the container, to brighten the home in winter with an unexpected reminder that spring can't be far behind.

The most important thing, before starting, is to make sure that the can you've selected has no sharp edges where the lid was removed. Ideally, you'll plan ahead for the project, saving smooth-edged cans till you have enough for each family member to make at least one container, several if they want. Wash each can and soak it in water till the label comes off. Dry it.

Now glue the candy canes to the outside of the can, all around, tightly against each other so the metal is hidden by the canes. (Alternative procedure: cut a piece of green crepe paper the right size to fit all around the can, and glue it in place, then glue four or six candy canes at regular intervals to the crepe paper, affixing them also to the top and bottom edges of the can for greater security.)

Now tie the ribbon around the canes, at about the midpoint of the can, finishing off with a pretty bow. You may want to put little dabs of glue under the ribbon in spots to help it stay in place better. A green ribbon is festively Christmassy against a solid background of red-and-white canes. If you've pasted the canes to green crepe paper, though, you won't want to use a green ribbon, because it won't show up well. In that case, silver or gold works better.

Candy Cane Hearts

Materials needed: two large candy canes, glue, four-inch red or white ribbon. (Optional: lace)

These hearts aren't for Valentine's Day but for Christmas— but of course, love is appropriate in any season. (Since they're made of candy canes, they could give new meaning to the expression, "Eat your heart out.")

They're so easy that everyone will want to get into the act. Just place two candy canes on a flat surface, facing each other so the two hooks are facing inward and will form a heart shape when joined. Then glue the spots where they're going to meet at top and bottom, pressing them together briefly so a good weld is created, and leave to dry. Tie a ribbon at the top, to hang the heart from the tree. You can also hang these on your front door or prop them up on your mantel.

Optional: Once the heart is glued, you can trim it with white lace, gluing the lace all around the outside for a Victorian effect.

Christmas Kindnesses

Materials needed: Christmas manger scene,
straw or hay or dry grass

If your family's Christmas celebration includes displaying a crèche or manger scene, and if the infant Jesus in your family's nativity scene is a separate figurine that's removable, you may want to institute this charming Christmastime tradition.

You'll need a supply of straw, hay, or dry grass. The amount will be determined by the size of your manger. A very small handful should do for the average-sized manger scene. If you don't have access to straw, hay, or dry grass in the wild, a visit to a pet store or garden supply store ought to turn up the material you need.

The point of the exercise is to provide the most comfortable bed of straw possible for the baby Jesus, whose figurine you will lay in the manger on Christmas. And the provision of the soft bed is the responsibility of the family members: The bed is created one straw at a time, the straws being put into the manger whenever a family member performs an act of kindness.

Each time a person is generous, suppresses selfish desires, or in some other way manifests the Christmas spirit, that person adds a straw to the manger. The acts of kindness are not discussed publicly, nor is each person supposed to be keeping count of his or her generosities or good deeds. The point of the activity is to give family members a chance to reinforce in themselves what is supposed to be habitual—the practice of behaving with kindness and selflessness.

Homemade Wrapping Paper

Materials needed: Newsprint, parcel-wrapping paper or butcher paper. For Variation 1: any of several textured surfaces to work on (see below) and several crayons. For Variation 2: fingerpaints. For Variation 3: pens, crayons, paints, or markers. For Variation 4: stamp pad and nonpermanent ink. For Variation 5: celery, inkpad (or paper towel and food coloring). For Variation 6: color comics saved from the paper, possibly scissors and paste or glue.

It would probably surprise a lot of people today to know that colorful wrapping paper has not always been something bought in a store. You can recapture some of the traditional fun of working together—and, not incidentally, save a lot of money!—by making unique, homemade paper for wrapping Christmas, birthday, or other gifts.

And if the gift happens to be for Grandma and Grandpa, how much more meaningful it will be to them if they know that grandson Ty or granddaughter Marcia made the paper himself or herself, as well as making or buying the present!

You may be able to get newsprint paper at an arts and crafts store; another source is your local newspaper, which will probably be happy to give you ends of rolls. Butcher paper can still be found in use by some independent butchers who aren't using supermarket shrink-wrap. And parcel wrapping paper is available at packing and shipping stores and many stationery stores, among other places.

Variation 1

Peel the paper wrappers from a variety of colors of crayons. Lay a blank piece of whichever type of paper you're using over a relatively flat object with an interesting texture or pattern. Some examples of these are: non-carpet welcome mats (especially the old hard rubber mud-scraper types), barbeque grills, a large number of coins lying on a flat surface, a piece of coarse-grained lumber, the plastic or metal grill over a window fan, the side of a big laundry basket, and the back or seat of a wicker chair.

Place the peeled crayon on its side and move it across the paper. A little experimenting will determine the ideal pressure to use and will show the variations possible by using various degrees of pressure. The paper can be colored in a single hue, in stripes of various colors, in rainbow arcs, or with one color laid over another after the paper has been moved slightly over the pattern-producing base. Whichever way you do it, the unusual pattern will be unlike any store-bought wrapping paper you've ever seen.

Each person can make several matching or similar pieces of

paper, or they can take care to make sure no two pieces of paper are alike. Variety within uniformity can be achieved by rubbing across the same surface with different colors or combinations of colors for different sheets.

Incidentally, using this technique on a piece of plain white typing paper, then folding the paper over, results in striking, individualized notecards.

Variation 2

Here's an utterly individualized and unique wrapping paper that may wind up carefully preserved, possibly even framed and hung, at least if Grandma is the recipient. Have the child creating the gift wrap coat his or her palm with a thin coating of fingerpaint, then transfer the paint and handprint to the paper in a random pattern, which can involve overlapping if desired, and can even involve two or more different colors.

Variation 3

Another form of personalized homemade wrapping paper that may find a second existence as a "Grandma's treasure" is accomplished by having the kids draw large and colorful pictures—using crayons, paints, or markers—appropriate to the season or occasion for which the paper is to be used.

If you're making the paper ahead of time, as a family crafts project, why not make some Christmas wrap, some birthday wrap, and some all-occasion wrap. For Christmas, of course, there are plenty of standard illustrations, from trees to stars to reindeer to Santa to holly wreaths and on and on. For Jewish families, or gifts to Jewish friends, menorahs and dreidels are certainly appropriate, as are Jewish stars. Birthday wrap might feature a cake with candles, cheerily wrapped presents, even kids playing party games. All-occasion wrap can also feature presents, smiling faces, and question marks indicating the mysterious nature of the contents.

The kids will love having large paper to draw on—they can draw B-I-G pictures, if they desire, though, of course, having lots of small reindeer or birthday gifts or whatever is perfectly appropriate.

Variation 4

A variation on the handprints-in-fingerpaint wrapping paper is to have the paper designers use a stamp pad (or several stamp pads of various colors), with *nonpermanent* ink, and make designs, patterns, or even pictures, using their fingerprints. By pressing her fingerprints in a circle, Laurie can create a rudimentary face, with one fingerprint representing each eye, one for the nose, and a small, semicircular row of fingerprints for the mouth. Billy might prefer geometric patterns—squares, circles, trapezoids, perhaps overlapping each other, and in different colors. And Rita might choose to make hearts out of her fingerprints. Or perhaps one of them will want to draw a more elaborate picture.

Variation 5

An unusual tool for printmaking—and for making unique wrapping paper—is a sliced piece of celery. Press the crescent shape of the flat end against an inkpad, or several pads of different colors, to use the celery as a rubber stamp, impressing crescents all over the paper in random patterns. In lieu of a store-bought inkpad, you can wet with food coloring a large piece of paper towel that's been folded over many times.

Variation 6

This colorful wrapping paper doesn't require any artistic talent whatsoever. You can save the color comics from the paper, using them as-is to wrap presents. However, you can also cut figures from the comics and paste them on brown paper or newsprint in random patterns, perhaps collage-style, using a light application of glue or paste. This is apt to get messy, between the glue and the newsprint rubbing off, but the result is colorful.

You can even create "themed" gift wrap from the comics. For a dog lover, for instance, cut out dogs from whichever comic strips run in your local paper, and paste just cut-outs of dogs on the paper: Farley from *For Better or Worse*, Snoopy from *Peanuts*, Marmaduke from the strip of the same name, Otto from *Beetle Bailey*, Daisy from *Blondie*, and whatever other dogs you can find in your paper's comics, even if they're just bit players and not regular characters. There are other themes you can find—winter scenes, flowers, odd-looking people...use your imagination.

The only drawback to comic strip wrapping paper is that it'll take twice as long to create as the other kinds if you figure in the time spent re-reading the comics before they're cut up!

Eggshell Mosaics

Materials needed: shells of dyed Easter eggs; posterboard, cardboard, or construction paper; glue. (Optional: tweezers or needle-nosed pliers, toothpicks)

Do your kids experience that old familiar letdown on Easter afternoon? The eggs have been found, the candy has been eaten, the holiday's over...there's school tomorrow. *Whap!* Reality hits them right in the face. And you have to listen to their grumbling.

Well, don't. Instead of letting them stew that it's over and they've nothing to look forward to in the way of holidays now till summer vacation, suggest they turn their Easter eggs into something special, something pretty, something they can make for Grandma or hang on their own walls—Eggshell Mosaics.

Carefully remove the shells from the Easter eggs, sorting them by color. While you whip up a batch of egg salad to pack for their school lunches, they can gather around the kitchen table making mosaics. Here's how: Crush the shells of each color into small pieces—no bigger than half an inch to a side (smaller is better). Pieces that are too large don't look as good and also tend to retain some curve, which is frustrating to work with.

On a rigid surface such as posterboard, cardboard, or construction paper, sketch the picture or shapes you intend to make into a mosaic. (If you're an experienced mosaic-maker and wish to skip this step and lay your shells down freehand, that's fine. All others are strongly encouraged to work from a sketched-in pattern.) If you wish, you can also note which colors go in which section.

Spread glue over a relatively small area; place your shell pieces in that area. When that section is complete, place glue in another section. You can put the shell pieces in place with fingers, tweezers, or needle-nosed pliers. Toothpicks can be useful for making fine adjustments to mosaic-piece placement after the shell is on the glued board.

(As the kids' fingers get gluey and shells start sticking to them, you'll get a fairly clear insight into the level of sophistication to which your kids' profanity vocabulary has developed!)

You'll be surprised at how artistic and professional even the most amateurish eggshell mosaic appears once it's complete. Certain kinds of art are very forgiving of lack of talent, and this is one of them.

Personalized Stories

*Materials needed: paper; pen or typewriter or computer,
possibly crayons or colored markers or paint,
construction paper, glue*

If your kids are a little short of money for gifts this
Christmas, or the next time one of their friends or cousins has a
birthday, they can still give a fine personalized present, created
just for the recipient. They can write a story *about* him or her.

In these computerized days, of course, it's possible for any
adult to buy a child a storybook in which is inserted the name of
the recipient, along with a few other details, such as, perhaps,
the name of the child's street, pet, and best friend. The thrill on
the part of the recipient is, in most cases, immense. But your
family can go the computerized books one better. Your family
can write a *truly* personalized story for cousins, friends, or
neighbors, written with the recipient's own interests and life in
mind.

Does your kids' Cousin Janey always wear pink bows in her
hair? Your kids can write a story about a girl named Janey who
always wears pink bows. No computerized book gets *that*
personalized.

Does your son's friend Mikey have a snail collection and a
terrarium full of assorted bugs, all of which gives his mom the
creeps? Your son can write a story about Mikey who has a snail
collection and a bug collection, and a Mom who gets the shivers
whenever she has to clean his room.

The ideal story would incorporate some details out of real
life, yet take off from there and soar off into the blue on a wild or
fascinating adventure or other intriguing story. If possible, it
should be illustrated (in crayon, paint, or marker, either on

parts of pages that are partially typed or written on, or on whole separate pages).

How long the story gets is entirely up to your kids. For that matter, whether it's a joint effort, family-written, or whether each child writes his or her own story is another question for discussion. If you have two kids, one good with words and the other artistic, let one write the story and the other handle the illustrations. If you have two kids and they have two cousins, one can write a story for one cousin and the other a story for the other.

If you think it's necessary or appropriate, you can jump in with hints, help, and suggestions, or type up the finished story. But if the kids want to present the story neatly handwritten, that's fine; it doesn't have to have a professional look. The idea here isn't to present a commercial-quality approximation of a book; it's simply to thrill a child with the most personal of personalized gifts, a story written *about him or her*, complete with real details.

If your kids absolutely cannot dream up a scenario for a story, they can still write a nonfiction account of a real incident in the life of the recipient. (Face it, even grown-up professional writers don't all write fiction. Many best-sellers are non-fiction. Many popular books are biographies.)

Did your son go camping with Mikey? Did your daughter organize a fantastically successful lemonade-and-comic-book sale with Janey? Let them tell the stories of these events, prominently featuring the other child, downplaying their own roles in the incidents. If your daughter can't dream up the story for "Janey Joins the Circus," she can still make a hit with "Janey's Successful Sale."

A variation on these books also makes a good present for a grandparent, aunt, or uncle. Here the suggestion is for the book to be about the child who is writing it, telling the story of his or her recent camp-out, appearance in a school play, or other real-life adventure. (If your kids don't yet know the terms "biography" and "autobiography," now's a great chance to teach them.)

They can tell the story as a narrative, or they can turn it into a comic book. The kids shouldn't attempt to cramp the pictures and writing into panels as small as those in the comics in your daily paper, though, or even those in comic books. Larger squares are much easier to deal with—even to the point of one square per $8\frac{1}{2}'' \times 11''$ sheet of paper, if need be.

In lieu of a recent experience the child has had and wants to tell Grandpa about, she or he might want to write about, or draw, the story of a previous visit with Grandpa (or whatever relative the story is being sent to). Did Grandpa come to visit (whether from across the country or around the corner) and take your son to the ballgame? Did they go camping together? Your child can recount the story for Grandpa, and Grandpa will surely keep it and treasure it as one of his best-ever presents.

When the book is finished, it can be enclosed between two pieces of construction paper for covers. Your kids can write the title on the cover in marker, ink, or crayon. Or, with greater effort, they can cut the letters of the title out of a contrasting color of construction paper, gluing the letters on. The whole thing can be stapled together, or punched with a hole-punch and secured with a fastener.

I said at the outset that these books are a good solution when your kids are short of money for gifts. But even if your kids' piggy banks are fat, they can still give a specially written story for a Christmas or birthday gift. The personalization, the thought that goes into such a gift is worth far more than money. The recipient will be thrilled by the thoughtfulness, the care, the uniqueness... and, in the case of a book for another child, the fact that the book is about him or her.

Holiday Home Decorating

Halloween candy turns into stomach aches and cavities; Valentines often wind up in the trash; July Fourth fireworks burn bright but disappear quickly. *Things* disappear. What remains from holidays is *memories*.

One way you can help make memories burn brighter than those Independence Day roman candles is to get the kids involved with you in decorating the house in a manner appropriate to whatever holiday is on tap. The festive air that the decorations will lend will be exceeded only by the enjoyment the kids will have in creating decorations with you.

Remember, Valentine's Day or St. Patrick's Day may not be a big deal to *you*, but for a kid these holidays assume a much greater significance. Valentine's Day can be right up there with the other biggies for some kids—my friend Vic's daughter was shocked, at an early age, to discover the school wasn't closed for Valentine's Day. It wasn't that she wanted the day off from school; it's just that she was disappointed to learn that this holiday didn't command the same level of respect as Thanksgiving, Christmas, and New Years, all occasions for closing the school. So make a big deal out of even the lesser holidays. Your kids do.

Holidays are an opportunity for learning as well as celebrating. As you decorate the house with your kids, take the chance to explain the holiday to them and fill them in on a little of the background.

Do they know why we eat turkey on Thanksgiving and sometimes even decorate the house with cardboard cutouts of turkeys?

Do they understand the significance of fireworks on the Fourth of July?

You needn't go to extremes. You certainly don't have to cut out construction-paper groundhogs to decorate your windows around February 2. And if you'd rather not have pilgrims and turkeys on your living room windows and walls in late November, or construction-paper-and-lace hearts in mid-February, your child's room can be the venue for such things. But surely you can place a gourd or two on your dining room table for Thanksgiving, and a wreath on your door for Christmas.

Seasonal decorations don't have to be tied to specific holidays, either. A cluster of varicolored fall leaves on a shelf or bookcase marks the passing of one season and the start of another, and is a good springboard to explaining the changing seasons to a small child. For a slightly older child, it's an opportunity to explain the tilt and rotation of the earth and its rotation around the sun. (Does your child know that in the United States we're actually nearer to the sun in winter, even though it's colder then?)

I don't suppose I need to tell you how to cut a Christmas tree out of green construction paper, or a Valentine's heart from red construction paper trimmed with paper lace (from doilies). But here are a few other holiday decorations you and your kids can enjoy making together. Or, if your kids are really young, you work on the project and let them watch you and discuss the holiday with you, then let them enjoy the festive atmosphere the decorations will engender.

Cheesecloth Ghosts

*Materials needed: cheesecloth; two cardboard rollers
from either paper towels or toilet paper; several short
lengths of coat-hanger wire; several balls, the size of
which will depend on the size of ghosts you're creating,
but might be tennis balls, handballs, ping-pong balls, or
even oranges; a stiffening solution for the cheesecloth,
which can be sugar water (for which you'll need
granulated sugar), or liquid starch (store-bought, either
pre-mixed or mixed at home), or a mixture of water and
Elmer's Glue; paint, or marker, or black construction
paper and paste or glue, or "googly eyes" purchased at
the crafts store. (Optional: monofilament fishing line)*

Start making your ghost by creating its arms, using coat-
hanger wire stuck through either a toilet paper cardboard tube
for a smaller ghost or a paper towel cardboard tube if you're
making a slightly larger ghost. Hold the cardboard tube vertically. About an inch down from the top, pierce the tube with
the wire, so it goes through into the tube and out again on the
other side horizontally. Stick it through till an approximately
equal amount of wire is jutting out on each side of the tube.
Stand the tube on a flat surface, with the wire sticking through
it, and place the ball or orange atop the tube.

Now stiffen your cheesecloth. If you're using sugar water,
dissolve as much granulated sugar in ordinary hot tapwater as
the water will absorb. Soak the cloth in the sugar water mixture.
If you're using liquid starch, mix it according to directions (or
use premix) and drench the cloth with it. If using Elmer's Glue,
mix it half-and-half with water and apply liberally to the
cheesecloth.

Now drape a doubled-over layer of cheesecloth over the ghost framework, shaping it to the head and outspread arms. Let it sit there and set till it has dried and stiffened. Slip the framework out and make as many more ghosts as you wish, following the same procedure.

Eyes and mouths can be made with paint, with markers, with pasted-on black construction paper, or even with crafts-store "googly eyes." If you wish, you can tape or glue a length of monofilament fishing line to the back or head of each ghost and suspend it from the ceiling, a light fixture, a curtain rod, or whatever opportunity presents itself.

Outdoor Ghosts

Materials needed: white sheet, pale solid-colored sheet, or other white or pale solid-colored material; newspaper, rags, or towels; twine, string, or light rope, or (preferably) monofilament fishing line. (Optional: more monofilament; marker, paint, or construction paper and glue, pins, or tape; length of light dowling, cardboard tube from wrapping paper roll, length of mop handle, or plastic baseball bat)

Ghosts floating in the air in your front yard can add an appropriately haunting flavor to your neighborhood as Halloween approaches, and making these sheeted visitors is one of the simplest and most basic family projects you'll set your hands to.

Just what you use for your yard ghosts will depend in part on the contents of your rag pile. If you have sheets ready to be turned into rags, great. If not, have you got white dishtowels you can do without for a week? Or large swatches of white material as yet not turned into that skirt or whatever you bought it for? If you have any of these, you've got it made. If not, you'll have to use a still-good white sheet (does anyone use white sheets anymore?), pale sheet, or other similar suitable material, working with it in a way that won't damage it for its post-ghost use.

The most basic ghost consists simply of a roundish head and a hanging body. Though simple and not very dramatic, it'll likely satisfy the younger ones in your family. Lay your material on the floor and place a head-sized bundle of rags, bunched-up towels, or crumpled newspaper in the center. Gather the material so as to wrap the stuff in the center you're using to form the head. Tie the ghost's neck with string, closing the packing in the head and leaving the rest of the cloth hanging free.

These ghosts can be made any size, from handkerchief-sized babies to full bedsheet-size behemoths. Hung from eaves, tree branches, porch railings, fences, or whatever else on your property presents itself as an opportunity, they can be a striking feature of your yard at Halloween time. When the wind moves them, their flapping and fluttering, especially in the semidarkness, can prove quite disquieting.

The mechanics of hanging the ghosts can be handled in any of several ways: String, twine, or light rope can be tied to the neck-defining string and used to hang the ghosts up. A more realistic flying appearance can be had by gathering a small knot, knob, or protrusion of ghost-sheet on the back of the head and tying string around that.

Further effect can be achieved by suspending the creatures from two points rather than just the head or just the neck. If your second point of suspension is most of the way down the body, and you pin the sheet together near the bottom, the ghost will appear to be flying as it hangs suspended virtually horizontally.

Rather than using string, twine, or light rope, you'll improve the illusion if you can get some monofilament fishing line. It's available at sporting goods or discount stores, if you don't happen to have a fully loaded tackle box in your basement. Since the thin, clear line is all but invisible, it will make the apparition that much eerier.

Ghosts with more substance can be created by adding some kind of arm-stiffener across the ghost's body, just below the head. Use a length of light dowling, the long cardboard tube from a wrapping paper roll, a length of mop handle, a plastic baseball bat, or anything else you have around the house that fills the bill.

Attach the arm-stiffener by tying a string around the inside-the-head material and allowing it to dangle through the tight-drawn closure of the neck. Then tie that end of the string around the middle of the stick to keep the stick in position.

If your ghost is constructed of a rag, rather than something that's facing an afterlife as a sheet again, you can use marker or paint to put features on your ghost's face. If your ghost-body is slated for reincarnation as your Thanksgiving tablecloth, however, you can still cut out construction paper eyes and mouth, taping them on, pinning them on with a small, thin safety pin, or even using a water-soluble glue.

For a more elaborate presentation, try stringing a line of monofilament from tree to tree, or lamppost to porch post, then hanging the ghost from the middle of the line, where it will appear to be suspended in midair. If you make several ghosts and suspend them from different lines of monofilament in different places, you'll wind up with a whole family of ghosts, hovering with intent to thrill.

Variation

If you have the kind of kids who are into benign mischief and don't mind crouching in the yard on a dark evening, there are various ways to manipulate your ghosts to make them appear "lifelike."

One involves stretching a more-or-less horizontal line of

monofilament high enough that the ghost can be suspended from it. Another piece of monofilament will attach to the top of the ghost's head or encircle its neck. The upper end of that piece of monofilament is tied into a loop around the horizontal line of monofilament, allowing the ghost to move back and forth along the length of the horizontal strand.

Another piece of monofilament extends out from the ghost's neck to the hand of a young prankster—your own real-life "monster"—who is crouched behind the bushes or some other suitable hiding place. From there, he can pull on the line to make the ghost move when an unwary pedestrian approaches.

Filigree Easter Eggs

Materials needed: oval or round balloons, liquid starch, food coloring, cotton crocheting thread. (If you have a wide assortment of colors of thread, or if you want a uniformly colored egg, the food coloring isn't necessary)

Filigree eggs are a delight on several levels, not the least of which is the satisfaction your family will have in making an object so delicate and beautiful with your own hands. Pride of craftsmanship figures large in this project, yet the eggs are relatively simple to make, and fun too.

Put the starch in a saucer. If you are using white crochet thread and dyeing it, mix the food coloring in with the starch in several different saucers, one for each color you want. Cut the thread into various lengths, from six inches to three feet.

Blow up a balloon and tie it off. Dip or soak a length of

crochet thread in the starch. Wrap the thread around the balloon, applying it in any direction—any swirl or pattern that appeals to you. Repeat with another thread, and another, and another. Let the threads overlap, loop, change directions, and go in whatever random pattern grabs your fancy.

The only concern is that the threads lie close against the balloon or the other threads; you don't want great sagging droops of thread anywhere. How heavily you apply the thread to the balloon will be governed by your taste and judgment. A general rule is that there shouldn't be any large gaps or holes in the crisscross pattern of the threads.

When you're satisfied with the thread pattern, hang the balloon up by its nozzle and allow it to dry overnight. When the thread is stiff and dry, pop the balloon. What remains is a remarkably delicate, intricate, and literally unique decoration. No two are alike.

Your filigree eggs can be hung in the window as home decorations for Easter, used as Christmas tree ornaments, or hung individually or in strings from a doorway for either holiday. Hanging them with silver or gold thread will add to their elegance.

Give filigree eggs as favors or prizes at parties or use them as part of decorative placecards at the dinner table. They make wonderful gifts, too.

5

Homemade Games

The array of games and toys available in stores is amazing and wonderful; and the high-tech special effects of some of those amusements would certainly boggle the mind of Buck Rogers. Yet, while taking nothing away from talking toys, video wonders, and high-tech gewgaws in general, there is a flip side to the extraordinary growth of manufactured toys and games. The tradition of families not merely playing games together but *making* the games they play has faded... and a lot of companionship, laughter, fun, and satisfaction has disappeared as a result.

Some of the simplest homemade games can provide hours of amusement for family members. The kids can play with each other, with their friends, with their parents, or alone. And they'll have the satisfaction of knowing they actually put the game together themselves.

Button Baseball

Materials needed: small box, carton, or box top; scissors; buttons, coins, washers, or similar small items; plain paper to cover the box or box top with and glue to hold it on, if the box isn't a solid, light color

The playing field for this "Minors' League" game is made from a small box, carton, or box top (standing on its lip). There are no league regulations requiring a particular size for the playing field! But an 8″ × 10″ field is about as small as you're going to want, while anything much above about 15″ × 24″ is going to be too large. The thin cardboard containers in which twelve or twenty-four cans of soda are packaged make good button baseball stadiums.

If the box or box top isn't plain cardboard color, cover the printing with typing, brown packaging, or similar not-too-dark plain paper. Now sketch a baseball diamond on the flat upper surface of the box. There is no regulation distance between bases; it will depend on the size of box or boxtop you're using. The important thing is to keep the drawn field in the familiar proportions of a real baseball diamond. Home plate should be near the bottom edge, first and third bases near the edges of the playing field. There should also be room for an appropriately proportioned outfield behind second base.

Cut circular holes at each of the bases, including home. The size of your playing field, as well as the age and physical coordination of your players, will determine the exact size you make the holes. As a general rule, holes between two and three inches in diameter are good; the larger the hole, the easier it will be to score.

Cut three more holes in the outfield, in roughly the positions that left, center, and right fielders would be playing. Draw base paths between the bases, a pitcher's mound, and a slender path between the mound and home plate. (These details are not necessary for play; they're aesthetic refinements, the home-made game's equivalent of a computer chip that makes the game croak, "Play ball!")

Label each of the holes as follows:

- The bases, first through third, are, respectively, Single, Double, and Triple.
- Home plate, left, and right field are labeled Out.
- Center field is labeled Home Run.

From a distance of five or six feet, probably while kneeling, toss large buttons toward the playing field. If no large buttons are available, you can use quarters, nickels, washers, or whatever similar tossable small objects offer themselves. The object, of course, is to make as many hits and runs as possible, and to avoid making outs.

A runner on base advances the same number of bases as the next hitter hits; that is, a runner on second goes to third when a single is hit; a runner on second goes home and scores when a double is hit, and so on.

More than two teams can compete in this game. If the players are Mom, Renee, and Bob, you have a three-team game, each team composed of one player. If there are many players, you can put two (or more) on a team, with each player on a team taking a turn in order.

Choose which team will go first, second, and so forth by any of the standard choosing methods: coin toss, "one potato," scissors-paper-stone, odds-evens, etc. There is no particular advantage to having first up or last up.

There are no strikes or balls in this most basic version of Button Baseball (see below for variations). Players advance according to the holes into which they sink their buttons (or other playing pieces). When a player has three outs, his or her side is retired and the next team comes up to bat.

It's not feasible to put markers on the field to represent base runners, because these might get in the way of tossed buttons. Among particularly contentious players, or if one or more members of the family are prone to fudging or have legitimately bad memories, keep a paper record of the number of outs and which bases have players on them to head off disputes. In less disputatious families, it should be sufficient for everyone to just remember that Renee is up, she has a runner on second and third, and one out.

Variations

- All holes on the field can be marked as hits (the three outfield slots as singles, home plate as a home run). In this case, a player is out when his or her button fails to drop through one of the holes.

• The field can be made with the various holes being different sizes; extra base hits can be harder to make because the holes are smaller than the holes for singles. The holes for Outs can be treacherously large.

• An extra hole can be added (perhaps out of the field of play, in the lower left or lower right part of the box, marked Walk.

• Instead of each player tossing for the batting team, each player can "pitch"—that is, the player represents the team *not* at bat, so the buttons are aimed for the "out" holes, just as a pitcher tries to throw the ball to compel the batter to make an out. In this version of the game, not hitting a hole cannot be an out, or the player would have no incentive to try to aim his or her button accurately. The best way, when it's a pitching game, is to declare the nonhole surfaces of the field to represent a pitch that is called a ball—four of those in a row, and the batter takes his or her base.

• Instead of tossing buttons or coins, the players can play using tiddlywinks. The place from which players play will, of course, be much closer to the playing field with tiddlywinks than with tossed buttons.

• The game can be played as a solitaire game, with the same player representing both teams.

• A Family League can be formed, if friendly competition and recordkeeping are to the taste of the family. Tournaments pitting each against the other can be arranged. In fact, more than one playing field can be created, with simultaneous games being played. Winners then play winners toward tonight's family championship, and losers play other losers in the consolation bracket.

Button Baseball may not be the most intellectually stimulat-

ing activity in the world, but it sure comes in a long way ahead
of most prime-time TV in that regard!

Egg Carton Skee Ball

*Materials needed: cardboard or foam egg carton;
posterboard or manila folder; handful of marbles or
ball bearings; crayon or marker. (Optional: tape)*

Even if the family can't get to a county fair or arcade, your
passion for Skee Ball can be satisfied at home, on a slightly
smaller scale... but without any charge for playing. An ordinary
cardboard or foam egg carton, a piece of posterboard or a manila
folder, and a handful of marbles or ball bearings are all that's
needed.

You may either cut off the lid of the carton or leave it on;
there's a reason for doing it one way or the other, which we'll get
to in a minute. Either way, though, do cut off the flap on the
nonhinge side of the box.

With either a marker or crayon, write numbers at the tops of
the backs of each cup in the carton. Try to write them so they're
visible to someone a few feet away from the carton.

Place the carton on the floor (or at one end of a long, empty
table). Tape the posterboard or one edge of the manila folder to
the front edge of the egg carton. This will serve as a ramp up
into the carton.

Place the whole rigged-up game on the floor or table where
you're going to be playing. If you want to provide extra stability,
a couple of pieces of tape holding the ramp to the floor can be
helpful.

From a distance of five or six feet, players roll marbles along
the floor or table, up the manila ramp, and into the cups of the

egg carton. Scoring is, of course, the number of points printed on the cup into which the marble rolls or drops.

Players each roll five marbles (or any other number that suits you), total their scores, and declare the round's winner to be the player with the highest score. Handicapping is accomplished by requiring that parents or older kids roll from a greater distance.

Now we'll deal with the carton's lid—on or off, and why. If the lid has been left on, it can serve a number of purposes. One possibility is for it to be used as a "dead tray." Marbles that fly over the cups and into it get no points. Or it can be the "default tray," providing a single point for any marble that ends up in it. Or it can be a tray with a negative point value, costing the player a point for every marble that winds up in it.

But if you don't plan to play by any of these rules, you may choose to simply lop the lid off beforehand. Before you do, though, consider that if players are consistently overly vigorous, and their marbles fly over the playing area and on down the hallway, or off the table, or wherever, the lid can come in very handy. What you want to do in that case is prop it up so it serves as a backboard.

Your family can carry recordkeeping and competition as far as seems appropriate or fun.

- Of course each game can be a self-contained competition in itself.
- If you want, you can arrange all-family competitions or tournaments, with the scores from many rounds being accumulated until there is a grand champion.
- You can also divide the family into teams, with partners' scores being added together in competition with the added-together scores of other teams.
- If you have a large family, you can even create "divisions," with tournament competition within each division resulting in a match between the division champions.
- If your family gets really good at the game, you can teach

it to other families and have interfamily competitions, with your whole family as one team competing against another whole family.

• And, last of all, this game, like so many others, is perfectly fun when played as a solitaire game.

Bottle Cap Basketball

Materials needed: ten soda bottle caps, wastebasket

This almost doesn't qualify as a family *project*, since no real construction is required for this homemade game. But since it *is* a homemade game, which is what we're dealing with here, and it's a game the whole family can play, I'm including it.

Really the only preparation required ahead of time is for various members of the family to have drunk ten bottles of soda, saving the caps. Also someone needs to empty a wastebasket. There—you're ready to play Bottle Cap Basketball.

Place the wastebasket in the middle of the room, or along a wall, or anywhere there's a free field of fire through which players can loft their bottle caps.

Players pitch, toss, shoot, throw, or otherwise propel their bottle caps, one at a time, toward the wastebasket, from a distance of about ten feet. Scoring can be two points per basket, to maintain the resemblance between this and the real game, or you can simplify matters and just score one point with each success. If agreed on by all players, a line can be established three feet farther away, with shots from behind that line being worth three points.

Play can be carried on in one of two ways: either each player at a time takes ten shots, the winner being the player who puts the largest number of bottle caps into the wastebasket; or players can alternate, each throwing one cap at a time, each holding his or her own ten bottle caps, till everyone has thrown all ten. Again, the winner is the player who sinks the largest number of baskets for the highest score.

Each round of ten caps can constitute a game by itself, or you may decide that a game is going to consist of ten rounds of play (or some other number). Since the game is very low-key, it's more an opportunity for companionship than a hotly competitive challenge.

And again, the game offers plenty of opportunity for solo play.

Spell Quoits

Materials needed: a piece of heavy-gauge cardboard or rigid foam insulation, or a piece of wood, plywood, or Masonite, approximately 18" × 26", possibly larger; twenty-eight cuphooks; heavy marker or crayon or paint; at least one eight-inch length of cotton or hemp clothesline (five or ten of them is better); masking tape or duct tape. (Optional: paint or varnish if you're using wood rather than cardboard or rigid foam)

Making a Spell Quoits gameboard can be as intriguing a project as actually playing with the thing. Whether you fashion an elaborate or a simple disposable one is entirely up to you, depending in part on whether you've got a family workshop and a handyperson in the family.

If you're going for the simplest construction, all you need is a rectangular piece of very-heavy-gauge cardboard—a piece cut out of the side of an appliance carton is perfect. The ideal size would be about 18″ × 26″. Larger is fine; smaller won't work as well. An alternative would be a piece of rigid foam insulation, the thickness of which should be at least a half-inch (three-quarters of an inch is preferable).

For a more elaborate construction, get a piece of wood of those same dimensions. Plywood works fine here, and Masonite is acceptable also. The wood may need to be trimmed to size, and you may want to varnish or paint it (if so, you won't be able to use it right away).

When the board has been cut, and painted or varnished if desired, screw twenty-eight cup hooks into the surface, with the hook upward. Space them out evenly, four across by seven down. You can determine placement as follows, if you like. Use a yardstick and measure, drawing lines. Leave a 3″ margin at the bottom and a 1″ margin on each of the other three sides. Now divide the width of the board into three equal sections and the height of the board into six equal sections. You'll wind up with eighteen rectangles of not quite four inches in height and just under six inches across. Screw a cup hook into each intersection of lines.

Now, using a heavy marker or crayon on cardboard, stiff foam, or untreated wood, or paint on a painted or varnished board, assign each hook a letter of the alphabet. It's generally best to go straight through the alphabet from upper left to lower right, though a random arrangement is workable too. With twenty-eight cuphooks and twenty-six letters in the alphabet, you'll have two hooks extra. You have two choices: leave both of them blank, or assign them both a duplicate letter ("E" is recommended due to the frequency with which it occurs in words).

The quoits themselves are easily made. Cut eight-inch pieces of cotton or hemp clothesline (slightly stiffer clothesline is preferable to limp). Bend each piece into a circle till the ends touch. Tape the ends together with masking tape or duct tape, and presto—you have quoits. Now, how many quoits do you need? You *can* play with just one; it's preferable to have at least five, maybe even ten.

There are various versions of Spell-Quoits. In each, the object is to toss the rope rings over the hooks corresponding to the letters you want to use to spell words.

Basic Spell Quoits

Lean the game board against a wall or sofa (truly vertical boards are hard to play on). All players together choose a word, then the first player stands perhaps four feet from the board. (The distance may need to be adjusted according to the age and abilities of the players; they should not stand so near that it's impossible to miss, but should be near enough that they have a fairly good chance of not only hooking their quoits but of getting them on the specific letters they're aiming for.)

This first player now aims for each letter of the target word, trying to hook the quoit over the appropriate letter in turn. The player continues till his or her quoit either hooks on a wrong letter or misses altogether, at which point, the next player gets a turn. When play comes back around to the first player, that person picks up where he or she missed last time.

For instance, if the word in question is *QUIET*, and Ann on her first turn had successfully hooked *Q*, *U*, and *I*, but then failed to hook the *E*, on her second turn she picks up at the *E*, trying to hook it and *T*. The first player to spell the word by hooking all the right letters in turn is the winner. A new word is chosen and a new round begins.

Pure Rotation Spell Quoits

Each player tosses only one ring per turn, and play circulates among all players. The letters of the word must be gotten in correct order. The first player to hook all of the letters in the target word, one letter per turn, in the correct order, is the winner.

Super-Tough Spell Quoits

To win at Super-Tough, a player must spell the whole word in one turn. If, to use the example in Basic, above, Ann had hooked *Q*, *U*, and *I*, and had failed trying for the *E*, in this version she would have to start all over when her turn came around again. Only by hooking all the letters in order in one turn can a player win.

Body Block Spell Quoits

This version assumes that the two extra hooks have been left blank. In this version, which otherwise follows the rules of Basic Spell-Quoits, above, the two blank hooks are "penalty" hooks. Any player who fears that another player is getting too close to completing the target word can "undo" that other player's letters by hooking one of the blanks after announcing, "I am undoing _____'s letters."

If the tosser—let's say it's Jerry—succeeds in hooking one of the two blank hooks, the opponent he named before tossing loses all his or her letters. There are three catches here. One: By using his turn to "body block" another player, Jerry gives up the chance to use his turn to increase his own letters. Two: If he fails to hook one of the two blanks, and instead hooks a letter or misses entirely, Jerry is penalized all of *his* letters. Three: If he succeeds, the player whose letters he is trying to take away may retaliate on his or her next turn and "body block" Jerry, tossing for one of the blanks to "undo" all of Jerry's letters.

Theoretically, the best time for a body block strategy is when you have no letters to lose and an opponent is close to winning. Should you hook one of the blanks, you're successful; should you fail, you lose nothing immediately, only risking reprisal from the other player. But the other player may be too intent on winning to give up a turn to body block you in retaliation.

Penalty Spell Quoits One

This version, too, requires two blank hooks, which in this case are designated as "erasers." Again, the rules for Basic are followed, but should a player accidentally hook one of the two blanks, all his or her letters are erased. (*Variation:* In a milder variation on Penalty, only the last-won letter is lost if a player inadvertently hooks a blank.)

Penalty Spell Quoits Two

Play follows the rules of Basic, above, except as follows: If a player's quoit falls on the floor, his or her turn simply ends, but if it hooks on a wrong letter, not only is the turn over, but the player loses his or her last-won letter as well.

Jokers Wild Spell Quoits

Again, two blanks are required. Following *either* the rules for Basic Spell-Quoits *or* the rules for Rotation *or* the rules for Super-Tough, the players are allowed to hook a blank at any time in lieu of any letter, the blank hook functioning as a "joker" and substituting for any other letter.

Box Quoits

Materials needed: boxtop or bottom of carton or piece of rigid foam insulation, about one foot by one foot in size; sharp object with which to punch or drill holes in it; ten or twelve wooden clothespins; marker or paint; clothesline and masking tape or duct tape, or, alternately, rubber rings used in home canning

Making the game board is a fairly simple project, but the game itself offers plenty of opportunities for fun. Punch or drill ten or twelve holes about half an inch in diameter with fairly regular spaces between them on the surface of the box top (or whatever you're using as a playing surface). Insert ordinary wooden clothespins into the holes so that they stick straight up. Write a number next to each peg, using marker or paint. (The simplest way to number them is from *1* through *10* or *12* in order, but any other method that appeals to you is acceptable.)

Make the quoits out of eight- to ten-inch lengths of fairly stiff clothesline, with the ends taped together with masking or duct tape, or you can use the rubber rings used in home canning. Kneeling four to six feet away, players toss their quoits, trying to make "ringers" over the pegs. They score points according to the numbers written next to each peg.

There are various ways to arrange a game. Each player can simply get five tosses. Or each player can get five tosses per round, with five rounds composing a game. Other methods are also possible. Players can compete on their own or in teams.

Round Robin

Each player is required to ring every single peg. The more demanding version of Round Robin requires that the pegs be ringed *in order*. If a player misses altogether, or rings the wrong peg, his or her turn ends and the next player's turn starts. When the first player's turn comes around again, that person picks up where he or she left off. If the player missed while trying to ring the 6, he or she now starts with 6 and keeps going till ringing all ten (or twelve) or missing again. The more relaxed version simply requires that they all be ringed at some point (in this case, pen and paper may be needed to keep track of which pegs a player has already ringed). A player loses a turn only by failing to ring any peg or by ringing a peg already ringed. The first player to ring all of the pegs is declared the winner.

Super-Tough Round Robin

In this version, appropriate only for very skillful—and patient!—Quoits players, the person must score every peg in order... and if she or he rings the wrong peg or misses altogether, not only does the turn end, but when it comes around to that player's turn again, she or he must start over from the beginning. In other words, in order to win, a player must ring *all* the pegs *in order in one turn*.

Call Shot

A player has the option of predicting which peg he or she is going to ring (it is *optional*, not required). If the toss is successful, the point total is doubled. If, however, the player rings a different peg he or she is penalized double the count of the peg ringed.

Death Peg

Any one peg is designated the Death Peg. Ringing it causes the player to lose all points. *Option*: If a player *calls* Death Peg (as in Call Shot) and successfully rings it, the opponent of his or her choice is stripped of all points. But if a player calls Death Peg and fails to ring it, he or she loses all points.

Topper Quoits

In this version, the player who plays first leaves all of his or her quoits where they drop. When the next player tosses, if any of that person's rings "top" the first player's scoring quoits, the score for that peg is deducted from the first player and transferred to the second player.

6

Learning Can Be Fun

Word Treasure Hunt

Materials needed: dictionary, paper and pen, possibly large slate and chalk

Here's a chance for your kids to get into a very healthy form of competition—and come out of it more knowledgeable. For this educational activity, there should be two or more kids, they need to be fairly close in age, and they need to be old enough to use a dictionary.

Each child is expected to come to dinner with a word in mind, a word the child doesn't think his or her siblings know. At dinner, each child presents the word of the day, pronouncing it, then waiting to see if any other child in the family knows the word. If a sibling can spell and define the word, the sibling claims a point, which is written on a scoresheet, or slate. If not, the child presenting the word spells and defines it. It would be a good idea for a parent to make note of the word on paper somewhere, but that paper should be kept hidden.

On the last night of the week, instead of each child presenting a new word, the kids are asked to remember all the words that have been presented that week—their own and their siblings. They are to write the words down, spelling them correctly and defining them.

You, referring to the list you've been keeping, verify the spellings and definitions if need be, awarding one point for each correct spelling and one point for each correct definition for each word for each child. Add those points to whatever points have already accumulated on the large piece of paper or slate. The child with the most number of points is the winner for the week.

Variation: A parent reads the week's new words aloud. The children are not expected to remember the words, only to be able to spell and define them.

Note that the kids are being asked to remember the new words introduced both by their siblings *and by themselves.*

A good dictionary is necessary for this game. It might happen that Pete brings a word to the table with one definition in mind and Fran already knows the word but knows a totally different, equally valid definition for it. A good dictionary, preferably unabridged, will settle the invitable arguments that will pop up.

Read 'Em and Reap

Materials needed: books, small piece of paper, pen, bowl

The poker expression is "Read 'em and weep," but I say, "Read 'em and reap," because of all the benefits a child reaps when he or she develops a love for reading. There are many ways to encourage this and some parents aren't above a little bit of bribery—or should we just call it "rewards"?

This project works only in a multichild household; if you have an "only child," move along to the next entry in this book. But if you have two or (even better, for this project) more kids, read on.

The idea is that you, the parent, promote a contest, in the form of a monthly drawing for some prize that all your kids would want. The kids get to enter the drawing once for each book they read during the course of a month.

- If Joan reads *Little Women,* she writes her name and the name of the book on a piece of paper, then drops it into a bowl.
- If she reads *Gulliver's Travels,* she writes *that* and her name on a piece of paper and drops in into the bowl.
- For every book every child reads through the month— *school assignments not included*—a piece of paper goes into the bowl.

At the end of the month, you close your eyes and dip into the bowl, withdrawing one piece of paper. The child whose slip you picked gets the prize. Dump out the rest of the slips and start over. The prize needs to be more substantial than a candy bar, yet not ridiculous. It has to be worth reading those extra books for, though, just in case love of reading isn't impetus enough.

If you suspect your kids may be cheating, not reading the whole book, you can ask for a brief book report to be "filed" with you when each slip of paper is deposited in the bowl. Or you can open the slips of paper before the drawing, ask random questions about the books involved, fold the papers again, deposit them back in the bowl, and have the drawing.

Regardless of who wins the drawing, all the kids are winners in that they've read a few good books that they otherwise might not have read. Read 'em and reap!

Bookin' Along

Materials needed: books

Few habits are more worth fostering, and confer more lasting pleasure on the members of a family, than the practice of regular reading. And one of the most effective and mutually rewarding ways for the members of a family to support and reinforce each other in this is to establish a regular pattern that involves not only reading but discussing the books each family member has read, and maybe even reading aloud some choice bits from the books.

Pick a regular time every week for Bookshare Night—or whatever your family wants to call it. Pick a time that's not claimed by a favorite TV show, a night when no one has Scouts or band practice or gymnastics, or a time during the weekend when nothing else is likely to clamor for the kids' attention and compete with book discussions.

If you make attendance at Bookshare Night voluntary, you want to make the prospect as appealing as possible. Not scheduling it at the same time as some competing tempting activity is more than half the battle.

If you make it compulsory, you don't want the kids to begrudge the time they spend discussing books they've read, squirming in their chairs, looking at their watches every three minutes to see if it's almost time for them to be set free.

If your family doesn't read voraciously, or their time is overbooked with outside activities, lessons, clubs, and whatnot, consider making Bookshare Night biweekly—better to do it less often than not to do it at all. But make a regular commitment, one that's reasonable for your family, and stick to it.

The activity is very simple. Each member of the family shares something about the book (or books, if he or she can't decide) that he or she has most enjoyed during the period since the last Bookshare Night.

No one is saying the kids have to write book reports—that's too much like school. All you're asking them to do is *talk*. Though, if they want, they certainly could write a book report or draw pictures...in fact, there are a number of activities that can be part of Bookshare Night, depending on the ages of the participants and their skills.

You can all concentrate on one of these activities, or each can do whichever activity best suits him or her, according to age, skills, and preference...for that matter, there's no reason for a family member not to participate in more than one of these activities.

- They can simply talk about the book, telling why they did or didn't enjoy it. (This makes them think about the book, about what they liked about it, about their own likes and dislikes, and about what makes a book a good book—at least for them.)
- They can pretend to be book reviewers and write a "grown-up, newspaper-style" critique of their chosen book for the week. Read them a few real examples of this form from the local paper to give them an idea of the format a book review is likely to take. Be sure to make the point once or twice—but don't overstress and oversell it—that the review you're asking for is not the same as a book review for school. In critiquing a book, your kids should give some thought to what makes a book good, to how a story is crafted, to what skills go into writing a good book.
- They can draw pictures of scenes from their chosen book.
- Two kids who've read the same book in the same week can act out a scene from the book together. Children who are into puppetry can even put on a brief puppet show

that depicts a scene from the book. If the child has a theatrical flair, and there's a suitable scene in the book, he or she can deliver a monologue in a very theatrical fashion.

• They can read aloud from the book, selecting dramatic passages, passages with great descriptions that evoke vivid mental pictures, funny passages, or whatever else appeals to them. This increases the ease and skill with which they read, particularly read aloud. It also is a basic building block to public speaking skills, which your kids may find useful in their adult lives.

You, too, can read aloud from the book you've most enjoyed in the past week. It may be beyond the children's reading ability, but that doesn't mean they can't comprehend select passages when they're read aloud. And if the kids *don't* understand what you're reading, help them with the "big words" and you'll be increasing their vocabularies.

Unless the best book you've read this week was a quantum physics textbook—or unless your this-week's reading was another look at *Lady Chatterley's Lover*—there's surely something in the book that the kids can appreciate.

The benefits from this activity are numerous. Bookshare Nights are an occasion for family togetherness. The activity fosters a love of reading, a good habit to get into and one of the better leisure-time activities. By critiquing the chosen books, or even just talking about them, the kids become more critical, not in the negative sense of the word, but in the sense that they'll learn to examine things rather than just accept them at face value. And by talking about, or writing about, what makes a particular book good, they'll get some insight into the craft of writing, a useful skill whether or not they have future aspirations in that direction.

If the family truly keeps to its schedule and gathers on a regular basis for the express purpose of sharing their excitement and enthusiasm about the books they're reading, a very fine foundation for a lifetime of reading will be established.

Journey Through the Encyclopedia

Materials needed: encyclopedia

There are various ways your family can make use of the encyclopedia above and beyond going to it for school projects or to look up answers to specific questions. Familiarizing the kids with the encyclopedia and how to use it will make them more comfortable using it, in turn aiding them in their school work, and later college work. It will also increase their general knowledge, another good thing. So get ready, get set... turn those pages!

This daily activity should take place at a regular hour— perhaps just before or after dinner. The family moves through the alphabet one letter at a time, one letter per day. Open the "A" volume the first day, the "B" volume the second, and so on. If your encyclopedia doesn't devote exactly one volume to each letter, you can choose to open each volume, in turn, rather than proceeding by letter. In any case, open today's volume at random, and focus on whatever entry is found on that page; if there are a few entries, choose one.

The members of the family are about to learn something. It may be in the field of geology, history, geography, biography, the arts... the possibilities are limited only by the information in your encyclopedia.

The kids will not only learn something of interest many evenings, they will also learn that knowledge is good for its own sake. You don't have to be faced with doing a paper in order to open the encyclopedia and learn what elephants eat, what Benito Juárez did for Mexico, or how British Somaliland and Italian Somaliland were merged to form the country now called Somalia.

It's probably best if each family member takes a turn in rotation, reading the encyclopedia entry. If Mom reads today and Dad tomorrow, Ian can read the next day and Joanne the day after. Then it's Mom's turn again. If there's time, and if the entries are short enough, each family member can read one entry in turn every night. If the kids aren't old enough to read the entries without stumbling over every other word, you can do all the reading.

If you turn to an immensely long article, you might want to skip it and page through to the next entry.

It's also a good idea for the family to discuss the entry that was read the previous night. This helps fix the information in everyone's mind. And if the family is the sort that enjoys quizzes and brainteasers, and you have the time, you can make up a quiz at the end of each week based upon the entries read during the previous seven days. Do present it as fun; it shouldn't take on the flavor of a school exam—more like a TV quiz show.

In place of the orderly, through-the-alphabet nightly dip into the encyclopedia, there are other methods for selecting the subjects to be learned each night.

- Write each letter from A to Z on a slip of paper and put them all in a bowl. Each night, someone picks a letter, and that's the volume from which you pick a page a random.
- Or one member of the family can call out a letter, another a number, and that page number in that volume is the target of tonight's search.

• It's also possible for family members to choose specific topics they want to read about on a given night. The positive aspect of this system is the guarantee that at least one family member will be genuinely interested in the topic; the down side is that you may find yourself spending night after night on different types of dinosaurs or planets, learning nothing about Mozart, rock formations, the various types of microscopes, or the different kinds of calendars that have existed over the centuries.

Sorting Around the House

Materials needed: objects encountered around the house

Are you the parent of one or more small children? Then you probably recognize the importance of teaching them sorting skills. But you don't have to buy them expensive toys to teach them to sort by shape, color, and other characteristics. In fact, even if they have toys that teach them to sort triangles from squares, or purples from reds, it's still good practice for them to learn to sort real-life objects.

No special equipment is needed. As you move around the house together, just ask, "Do you see any rectangles in this room?" or "What do you see that's blue?"

With a little help and a few hints, your kids will soon recognize that the living room carpet is brown, the curtains in their room are blue, the kitchen towels are yellow, and the skirt you have on today is red.

They'll begin to recognize shapes around the house too, picking up the fact that the top of the coffee table is a rectangle, your round watch is a circle, the cake pan is a square, and their toy triangle is literally that—a triangle.

After they've mastered distinguishing among the various shapes and colors, you can start introducing other concepts into around-the-house searches: hard and soft, large and small, even things found high and low.

Go-Togethers

Materials needed: objects found around the house

Along with sorting, your very young child needs to learn grouping, another activity you can get into just going around the house. If your child has an older sibling, the sibling can become involved and feel important playing "teacher" to his or her younger brother or sister.

The object of grouping is for your child to recognize things that belong with other things—things that fall into groups. Tables, chairs, and lamps are all *furniture*.

- Knives, forks, and spoons are all *utensils*.
- The poodle next door and your golden retriever are both *dogs*.
- Your dog and your other neighbor's cat and your cousin's goldfish are all *pets*.
- Hamburgers, steak, pork chops, and ham are all *meat*.
- Celery, green peppers, lettuce, and peas are all *vegetables*.

• Peaches, apples, and pears are all *fruits*.
• And all these last three groups—meats, vegetables, and fruits, are, along with other items, *food*.

Make a game of it. Go around the house together, you and your young child, and ask how many things she or he can find that belong in groups. Even if Mary doesn't know a name for the group two or more items belong to, praise her for identifying the objects as go-togethers.

If your child can't find go-togethers alone, or if he or she doesn't know the names for the groupings, this activity can be initiated by your saying, "Honey, you know that a lamp is a piece of *furniture*, right? Can you show me what else in the house [or in this room] is furniture?"

The child can play this game with either parent or with an older sibling. . . perhaps one who at one time participated in this very same activity with you, and not that many years ago.

Cuddly Letters

Materials needed: felt or other nonfraying fabric, in two different colors; stuffing (such as foam rubber pieces or cotton stuffing); needle and thread; paper (preferably graph paper); pencil

Your child will not only learn the alphabet but love it when it's in a cuddly form. And what could be softer than a fuzzy felt letter fatly stuffed with foam?

Unless you're super-self-confident about cutting the letters out freehand, you'll want to trace a pattern for them on paper.

Graph paper will give you straight lines to guide you and is your best option. Trace the letters of the alphabet—capitals or lower case or both—on paper, using a pencil and erasing if you're not happy with the results. About three inches high is a good size.

Now hold the paper stencil you've created up against the felt and cut, once on each color of felt. It's best if you cut the "fronts" of all the letters out of one color, and the "backs" out of the other. This way your child will always know the letters go "blue side up" or "yellow side up."

While you will be doing all the cutting and sewing yourself, of course, your child can watch while you work, and you can say, "I'm sewing an A, I'm sewing a B now," and so forth. Sew right along the edges of the outsides of all the letters. Use even stitches and a contrasting color thread for a decorative effect.

It will be easier if you stuff as you go along. For instance, on a capital B, sew the back (left side) of the letter from the middle down, and then the bottom; stuff the part you've sewn and resume sewing, stopping when you're part-way up to stuff more, and so on.

Your part of this project may take a while, especially if you're not a person who is accustomed to crafts or creative sewing, but your child isn't going to learn his or her alphabet all at once, either. So it's fine if you sew a few letters, give them to your child, and sew a few more while she or he is learning that the first three are A, B, and C. (If your child has a short first name, you can opt to sew the letters of his or her name first, instead.)

Your child will now have cuddly, colorful letters to play with, snuggle with, and learn the alphabet from.

Language Lessons

Materials needed: paper, pen, tape and/or safety pins

Do you have a child who's old enough to read? Does his or her school teach a foreign language to their kids? Do you speak a foreign language?

If you answered yes to the first and third questions—even if the answer to the second was no—you can increase your child's knowledge of a foreign-language by familiarizing him or her with the words for everyday objects. Pin or tape a large piece of paper that says *LA SILLA*, for example, to the chair in your child's room (or any chair in the house), *LA MESA* to a table, *LA PUERTA* to a door, *LA VENTANA* to a window, and so forth.

Color names, too, can be taped or pasted to appropriate objects.

- Is the color of your fridge *AMARILLA*? (It's *amarillo* for male yellow objects, but a fridge is *una nevera* and requires the female form of the adjective.)
- Is her *BICICLETA* (bike) *ROJA* (red)?
- Is the cover of his favorite *LIBRO* (book) *VERDE* (green)?

Of course, if the language you're giving your child a head start in is being taught in school, so much the better—he or she will be a jump ahead of the rest of the class. But even if not, the knowledge won't hurt. If the elementary school doesn't teach foreign languages, or not the one you know, chances are it'll be available in high school.

Even if she or he elects to study a different language, knowing the names for objects and colors may spark an interest in learning more of the language, either from you or from someone else who speaks it. (You could even hire a local high school or college student who's fairly proficient in the language to tutor your child.) And the knowledge will stand your child in good stead as she or he goes through life.

¡Buena suerte!

The Rock 'n' Roll Waltz

Materials needed: none, although a piano is helpful

Do you remember the song of a number of years ago, "The Rock 'n' Roll Waltz," in which parents were trying to waltz to a rock beat? How familiar are your children with the concept of 2/4 time, 3/4 time, 4/4 time, 6/8 time, etc?

How familiar are you with the various time signatures? If you have a grasp of music fundamentals, you can explain to your kids that waltzes are written in 3/4 time, marches and many other kinds of music (including much in rock) in 4/4 time, syncopated rhythms have an off-beat, and all these factors influence the way music sounds.

Now take a song the kids recognize, whether it's a popular rock song or "Twinkle, Twinkle, Little Star," and try singing it in 3/4 time, effectively turning it into a waltz. If you have a piano, you can incorporate that into your demonstration. Play around with a few different songs, singing or playing them in 2/4 time, 3/4 time, and 4/4 time, and syncopating them too, so your kids can hear the difference.

Now let your kids try the same thing. Never mind if you all sound silly. Relax and have fun turning "Mary Had a Little Lamb" into a bossa nova, or the ABC song into Dixieland jazz.

Around the World
Around the Table

Materials needed: possibly an encyclopedia or globe

The exact form this activity will take depends on the ages and interests of your children. The point of it is that too many kids grow up far too ignorant of geography, both world geography and American. And what better time than dinner, when the family is all together, for you to impart a little geographical knowledge to them—or for them to impart it to each other.

If your kids are little, it may be enough to pepper the dinner conversation with tidbits of knowledge:

- The capital of New York isn't New York City; it's Albany.
- Flemish is the language of Flanders and is one of the official languages of Belgium.
- There are eleven time zones in Russia.

If your kids are a little older, you can get into more extensive material and ask them to provide it. Perhaps once a week, so it doesn't become an odious burden, each child can be asked to prepare three minutes' worth of information on any location on the map. The information can be garnered from the encyclopedia, a library book, or any other suitable source.

If you have an old, outdated globe or atlas, you can bring it to the table and show the rest of the family the countries that aren't there anymore.

- East and West Germany have been unified into one.
- Cambodia is now Kampuchea.
- The U.S.S.R. is nonexistent as such.
- Depending how old your map is, you might be able to

show them Siam, Persia, and other longer-gone country names.

Whatever form your geographical wanderings take at the dinner table, your kids are bound to get up from the table with their brains as well as their stomachs enriched.

Big-Game Book Safari

Materials needed: reference books (library books are fine), paper and pen

If you've got two or more kids, here's a way for them to engage in a little healthy competition that's educational. Send them on a safari... but nobody's going to get lost in the jungle or stuck in the mud. They needn't venture any farther than the shelf on which you have your encyclopedia, or the public library, with all its reference material.

Here's how it works: Offer a modest prize to the child who "captures" the most animals on his or her safari. To capture an animal, the child has to list five facts about it, or, as a variant if you prefer, write a half-page essay about it.

You can, if you wish, make it a rule that cats and dogs, or all common house pets, are exempt from the safari. This will prevent a child from getting credit for turning in a list of common facts such as:

1. Cats have fur.
2. Cats purr.
3. Baby cats are called kittens.

4. Cats like to drink milk.
5. Milk should not be fed to adult cats.

The kids should have to do some looking-up of facts in order to take credit for capturing an animal.

If the kids are enthusiastic, do a decent job of coming up with animal facts, and seem to have learned something, repeat the safari at a later date, requiring them to come up with different animals than before. (You might want to accept Irene's doing a report on an animal Aldo previously "captured," as long as she doesn't repeat a report she herself previously gave. You could even decide to allow Aldo to report on an animal he previously "captured," as long as he reports different facts this time.)

Good luck, big-game hunters. Bring 'em back alive.

Camera Safari

Materials needed: camera, encyclopedia or other reference books (library books are fine), paper and pen

Another kind of safari your kids can go on involves using a camera. If they have cameras—simple, inexpensive ones will do—all they have to do is snap a picture of an animal (pigeons count, as do squirrels, whatever wild animals live in your area, and even domestic pets, as well as whatever's on display at your local zoo). The picture doesn't have to be great photography; the animal just has to be recognizable.

Step two involves a trip to the library—or to the reference shelf at home, if you have an encyclopedia or other reference books. There have the child look up facts on the animal he or she has snapped the picture of, and pasting or gluing the picture to the top of a sheet of paper, write up a brief summary of the facts learned below that.

If it's a common animal, such as a dog, urge your child to avoid the obvious ("Dogs bark") and stick to facts she or he didn't already know. There are plenty.

Unlike the Big-Game Book Safari, above, this one's not a competition, so it's as suited to an "only" child as to one with siblings.

If the child wants, he or she can even make an album or "book" out of the reports, with construction paper covers.

Rhyme Time

Materials needed: none, except possibly pen or pencil and paper

Kids love rhymes—from the earliest nursery rhymes to Dr. Seuss's books and beyond, through the rhymes used in play. Some games are set to rhyme, such as those accompanying rope-jumping or various ball-bouncing games, and if you listen to little kids who think they're alone and unobserved, you'll sometimes hear them singing nonsense rhymes to themselves.

But they don't all think about what they're saying. If you ask a small child, "What rhymes with banana?" she may not immediately answer "Anna" or even the imperfect answer, "piano." Some degree of conscious thought is required.

It's not, however, the kind of thinking that kids mind. Asking, "How many words can you think of that rhyme with 'feet'?" is not like quizzing a child on his or her times-tables. Got ten minutes to kill? See how many rhymes a child can think of for "table" or "chair." (It's OK to give clues or hints...though after a short while, you probably won't have to give very many. Kids get the hang of thinking of rhymes quickly.)

You can even have rhyme contests. If your kids are old enough to write, sit them down and give them each one minute, or three, to think of as many rhymes as they can for "head" or "small" or "bear." (If they're old enough, you can detour briefly to explain what a homonym is, and why "bare" is not a rhyme for "bear" even though they're two different words.) The winner is the one who thinks of the most valid rhymes for the word you've supplied.

If the kids are really getting into it, you can even ask them to create simple poems. (Also see Limericks, page 192.) The meter doesn't have to be perfect, and if the poem is only two short lines, that's fine, too. Praise their efforts if they're at all praiseworthy. You may have the next Robert Frost (or a potential Grammy-winning lyricist) under your roof...but even if they only write for their own or their family's amusement, what a great gift.

I had two aunts who were beloved in the family for their poems. My childhood birthday cards from Aunt Esther and Aunt Hank (Hanna) were as likely to contain home-crafted verses as Hallmark's—and since the home-crafted ones often had my name written into them somewhere, I infinitely preferred them to store-bought cards. Your kids, too, could become the family's poet laureates.

Start them out by asking them to supply rhymes for simple, one-syllable words. Who knows where it could go from there? But even if they never become famous for their well-crafted poems, they'll have fun with "bear-where-care-dare-fair-lair-snare-tear-rare-mare-stare-air-pair." So there!

7

Serious Stuff

Emergency Rehearsals

Materials needed: list of emergency phone numbers

One of the most worthwhile projects your family can undertake isn't a fun project but a most necessary one: rehearsing for emergencies. The rehearsals can take the form of actual runthroughs or simply verbal descriptions of what to do, but your kids need to know what the best procedures are in case of various types of crises that can arise.

Perhaps you say, "My children are never home alone," but even so, they need to know what to do just in case of that one exception. Or suppose something happened to *you* while you were home with the kids, either an illness or an accident, and you became unconscious. Would the kids know what to do?

One of the first things you need to do is post a list of emergency phone numbers next to a centrally located phone (preferably next to *every* phone). These should include:

- Fire—911 (unless it's different in your community)
- Police—911 (unless it's different in your community)
- At least one immediate neighbor the kids can call
- Work numbers for working parents
- Poison control
- Your doctor
- Your kids' doctor
- Any other relevant emergency numbers

Now run through the procedures in case of various emergencies and other situations that require calm, quick thinking—and repeat the drill *at least twice a year.* They should know what to do—whether or not you're home—in the following cases:

- Fire when a child is alone in the house
- Fire when someone else is home with him or her
- A stranger is at the door
- An intruder is trying to get into the house
- An intruder is already in the house
- Earthquake, if you live in a quake-prone region
- Tornado, if you live in a tornado-prone region
- Another person choking
- An unconscious parent and no other adult in the house
- An interior flood caused by a plumbing emergency when no adult is in the house
- A phone call from a stranger asking questions when no adult is in the house
- A downed electrical wire in the vicinity (the instructions for this one should include not only avoiding the wire itself but also avoiding anything that might be touching it)
- A gas smell in the house (in addition to whatever other instructions you give them, make sure they know not to turn on any lights or other electrical appliances if they think they smell gas)
- Any other emergency situation you can think of that your particular children might possibly encounter with or without your being present
- In addition, if you, your spouse, or any of your kids has a medical condition such as epilepsy, diabetes, or severe allergies, which could cause seizure, coma, or shock, make sure all your kids know what to do should they find the affected person in such a medical crisis.

With regard to fire emergencies, you should physically lead

your kids out every door that might be used as a fire exit. If you have windows that open completely out of the frame for fire exits, make sure the kids know about this and know how to push the window out. They should also know how to operate your fire extinguisher (and if you don't have one, get one... *now!*).

Try to be reassuring in your presentation of these rehearsals; you don't want to frighten the kids and overwhelm them with awful possibilities. On the other hand, you *do* need to be sure they know what to do if one of these situations arises. Tell them that if they know what to do in an emergency, it's like wearing a protective suit of armor (or some other simile they can relate to). Remember, rehearsals can save lives!

Disaster-Avoidance Rehearsals

Materials needed: none

Along with the Emergency Rehearsals, above, for crises in the home, you should also run through rehearsals with your kids for other types of situations in which a quick and appropriate response is vital. These situations range from being bullied and beaten up to being molested or the victim of an attempted abduction.

Start with the most common and likely: Would your child know what to do if another child bullied him or her and threatened to beat him or her up? How you'd want your kids to deal with this situation may not be how your neighbor or best friend would want his or her kids to handle it, and I'm not attempting to give advice here. *You* need to decide what you think the best response is. But whatever you decide, impart that information to your kids.

At the very least, talk through the situation: "And then this bully says, 'I'm going to beat up on you' and swings his fist near your nose. What do you do?" Even better, perhaps, role-play the situation. Pretend you're the bully. Menace your child. Elicit a reaction. Correct him or her if the response is not the one you'd like.

Now what if another child actually does beat up on your child? What should she or he do? This is different from mere bullying. Discuss the possibilities. Do you believe in fighting back or seeking help or running away? Explain why telling an adult isn't "tattling." What should the child do if he or she responds by fighting back and the other child gets the best of him or her? What if the fight takes place on the way to or from school and the child is hurt badly? Should she or he ring a stranger's doorbell, or is there another response you'd prefer?

What if a child is stopped by an older child who mugs him or her for his or her lunch money, or whatever other money your child has? You would probably advise your child to give up the money to save bloodshed, and then to report the incident when she or he gets to school. But whatever your response, make sure your kids know what you want them to do should this circumstance ever happen to them.

Another situation they need to be prepared for is a stranger stopping them on the street and asking them questions. For younger kids, "Don't talk to strangers unless you're with one of us and we say it's all right" may suffice. For kids a little older, some differentiation is needed. You may feel it's all right for them to answer, "Which way is Elm Street?" but the kids should know not to tell a stranger where they live, what their names are, or other information like that.

One step up in the realm of dangers: Remind the kids never to get in a car with a stranger. I'm sure you've told them before, but have you told them recently? Have you rehearsed possible scenarios with them? Pretend you're a stranger and say to them, "Your mom told me to give you a ride. She's waiting for you at the ice cream store," or something like that. Make sure they wouldn't fall for such a ploy.

Now let's take another serious problem: inappropriate touch. In this day and age you need to tell your small children where it's not appropriate for other people to touch them, and in what ways it's not appropriate for others to touch them. Explain about private parts of the body. Tell them that if it ever happens to them, it's nothing for them to feel guilty about, but they need to tell the other person to stop, and they need to report it to you immediately.

Tell them, too, that people who touch like that can also threaten, and if the person says, "Don't tell or I'll do something bad to you" (or "to your Mommy" or whatever other threat), they aren't to let that frighten them. You'll protect them. You won't let the person hurt them, you, or any other family member. And reporting the incident to you isn't "tattling," either. They need to tell!

Don't say, "It could never happen to my kids," or "It could never happen in my family." It happens to the nicest kids and in the best of families. I hope it never happens to yours. But if it does, your kids need to be prepared to handle it.

Are there other situations you can think of that your children need to be aware of? Protect them by rehearsing, or at least running through it verbally with what-ifs. Reassure them that these situations aren't likely to arise. Try not to scare them unduly... but remember that scaring them is less harmful than the alternative—that such a situation should arise and they don't know how to handle it. Then hope with all your heart that your kids never need the information you're giving them... but know that you've prepared them well, just in case. And run through these rehearsals at regular intervals—say, every six months.

This family project isn't the least bit fun. But it could save a life, or at least an awful lot of heartache.

The Giving Family

Materials needed: possibly some large cartons or shopping bags

The concept of charity—doing for others—is an important one, and one that most of us try to instill in our kids at an early age. There are three things a person can give: time, money, effort. A child old enough to understand that some people are less fortunate than others is a child old enough to do something for some of those people.

And the whole family can get involved in the project.

There are lots of possibilities:

- The family can call on seniors in a nursing home, people who have no family, or no family nearby, and don't get visitors. You can visit area nursing homes, going to a different one each time, or you can "adopt a grandparent" and visit that one person every time.
- Around the holidays, you can all go out collecting food for families who otherwise might have bare Thanksgiving or Christmas tables. For that matter, if there's a food bank or similar organization in your community, you can go out and ring doorbells for monetary or food contributions

any weekend, donating the proceeds of your efforts to the organization.

- The kids could offer to give a very small portion of their allowance every week or month to a worthy cause. You can have them drop their coins in a charity's collection box in a local store, or you can start a special savings account or piggy bank (under your control!) for the purpose of saving money for charity. After a suitable interval—say half a year—withdraw the money, get a money order, and send the contribution to a charity you've all agreed on. (Watching the money mount over the weeks may be an incentive to the kids to learn to save some of their allowance for themselves, too, seeing how it adds up when they're diligent.)
- Is there a child in school who has a disability—CP, MS, MD, or even a milder affliction that doesn't usually get thought of as a disability but still has an organized association doing research on the condition? This might make the contribution more meaningful for the kids. If Mitch who goes to their school has cerebral palsy, the kids can donate their money to United Cerebral Palsy, knowing the contribution will—in whatever small way— help the Mitches of the future have less of a hassle, less of a disability...or maybe be spared of putting up with the condition altogether.
- Does your church have a soup kitchen for hungry local residents? The kids can work there once a month, doling out food or even washing dishes, if they're old enough.

Whether the kids give time, money, or work, whether they give money to an organized charity or simply make an effort collecting used clothes or canned goods for less fortunate people locally, whatever form their efforts take, they'll have the satisfaction of knowing they've helped make a difference, however small, in improving the world and the quality of life for someone. And, if the family works on the project together, you'll feel a sense of being united in purpose, working together for this very good cause.

Charity Begins at Home

Materials needed: kids' rooms overfilled with toys and games

"If he didn't have so many toys, it wouldn't be so hard for him to keep his room clean—and he never even plays with half the stuff anymore." Sound familiar? Maybe Christmas or a birthday is coming, and you're dreading the fresh influx of toys and games on top of too many already. Maybe you've got spring cleaning on your mind, but even you feel daunted by the prospect of attacking your child's room with so many goodies in it, goodies that are largely going to waste.

It's time to do something about it.

True, most kids rebel at the vague, ambiguous concept of giving toys away "to charity." Even if there's a Goodwill box or similar charitable collection point and your children know the toys are going into the box, they probably don't have a clear idea of what happens to the toys after that.

You can instill a liking for charitable deeds in most kids. And you can get rid of some of the clutter at the same time. But you have to put a face on the charity. Suggestion: Instead of just talking about giving the toys "to charity," pick a few specific charities that your child can relate to, make the charity a tangible entity, and offer your child some options.

In or near your community, there are probably several of the following:

- A home for orphans
- A shelter for abused kids
- A nursery or hospital or home for kids with AIDS
- A hospital for other seriously ill kids
- A collection program for toys for needy kids

Explain these charitable organizations to your child. Describe the situation of the kids who benefit from them. Decide on a reasonable number of toys or games you can expect your child to give away (let's say ten, for argument's sake). Now tell your child that she or he has a choice of which ten toys to donate and also a choice of which of these organizations is going to receive them.

If it's feasible, take your children with you when you donate the toys, so they can more keenly feel involved in the actual process—the toys aren't just whisked away by mom to mysteriously disappear in the car after the selection is made. The kids probably won't see any of the actual beneficiaries of their charity, just an office, but they'll still feel more actively involved and will relate more specifically to what's going on.

Your child will be on the road to acquiring the habit of giving to charity, some children somewhere will be made happier by his or her contribution, and you'll face less clutter in that disaster area known as your child's room. It's an everybody-wins situation.

Reaching Out

Materials needed: a small financial contribution from each family member every week

There is no end to the list of ways that a family can reach out and make itself felt in the life of another person or family. Some possibilities are discussed in The Giving Family and Charity Begins at Home, above. Another way to be of help where help is needed is by giving regular financial aid to a particular child or family in need.

There are any number of organizations that provide financial assistance to children or families either in the United States or in foreign countries. Many of these organizations will provide the donor with periodic letters from the individual or family receiving the help.

Of course, before you get involved with such an agency, you should check it out and make sure you are sending your money to a legitimate charitable organization and not a scam. Check with your state's Secretary of State. One charity that has been recommended to me as a hundred percent legitimate, reliable, and trustworthy is WorldVision, in Monrovia, California. But it is by no means the only such worthwhile organization.

Your family will be asked to contribute an amount of money at regular intervals. For this to be meaningful to your kids, the money should not all come out of *your* pocket. Each of your kids should commit to contributing a set amount on a regular basis—even if it's only ten cents a week. Obviously, what constitutes an appropriate amount will depend on whether we're talking about a very small child with a fifty-cent-a-week allowance and no other income, or a fifteen-year-old who gets an appreciable allowance *and* cuts lawns or baby-sits or delivers papers for extra money.

Not only will contributing money regularly get them started on the path toward being charitable people, the letters your family will receive from the child you're sponsoring will be meaningful and educational for your kids. They may complain about not having a Nintendo game, or as many Game Boys as their friends, but when they start receiving letters from a child who has no shoes, or only two sets of clothes, or who feels lucky because he or she got two full meals yesterday, your kids are going to look at their own "deprivations" in a new light.

Breaking Barriers

Materials needed: pictures, either cut from magazines and newspapers or drawn, of different children of clearly different ethnic and social backgrounds

It's true that, as the song from *South Pacific* goes, "You've Got to Be Taught" to be prejudiced; kids aren't born mistrusting people whose skin is a different color, whose eyes slant differently, or who wear a different religious symbol around their neck or even dress "differently." But prejudice is so pervasive that kids can pick it up at an early age. You aren't the only person who comes in contact with your child. Kids can acquire unwanted attitudes outside your family circle. Unless you send out strong signals of equality at home—and sometimes even if you do—kids can begin at very young ages to be aware of the differences in people, and to mistrust or dislike people who are different from them.

Of course the best way to combat prejudice in your children is by example. Live a life free of prejudice, have friends of various ethnic backgrounds, and don't use ethnic slur words or speak derogatively of any group. But sometimes that isn't enough. Sometimes you have to take positive steps to combat the negative input your kids get on the outside.

One way to combat these prejudices is by cutting an assortment of pictures from newspapers and magazines, trying to find pictures of children from as many different ethnic backgrounds as you can, such as:

- Black
- White
- Asian
- Hispanic
- Native American
- East Indian
- Eskimo

You might also want to include pictures of:

- A child in a wheelchair
- A child who lives in obvious poverty and dresses accordingly
- Any other stereotypes you feel your child might have acquired negative beliefs about

Now ask questions such as:

- "Which do you think is the nicest child?"
- "Which do you think is the least nice child?"
- "Do you think any one of these is a 'bad' child?"
- "Which of these kids do you think you'd most like to be friends with?"

Ideally, the child should answer, "How can I tell? I don't

know any of them." Ideally, yes, but we don't live in an ideal world. In all probability the child will be drawn to a picture of a child who looks like himself or herself—same ethnic background and probably same sex. Quite possibly he or she will identify that child as the nicest. Now ask, "Why do you think that child is nicest?"

Show the child that she or he was making false assumptions based on ethnic background. Explain that a person isn't better or worse just because he or she is black/white/Latino or whatever. Mention a friend of yours or your child's who is from a different ethnic background, and say, "Don't you think _____ is a nice person? She's [black/white/Eskimo/Hawaiian/whatever]." Get into a discussion about prejudice (including explaining that it means "pre-judgment").

And examine your own attitudes and speech to make sure your child isn't picking up bad attitudes from *you*.

Family Council Meetings

Materials needed: none, or possibly pen and paper

"Because I said so." That's the answer old-fashioned parents used to give when kids challenged a command with "Why?" Nowadays, few parents rule with such an iron fist. Most are willing to give a reason when questioned, at least most of the time. In general, families are run more democratically than in our grandparents' day.

And right in line with a democratic family is the Family Council. Whether meetings take place once a week or once a month, the idea is for the family members to sit around the living room, the family room, or the kitchen or dining room table and talk about their requests, their needs, their grievances, and any disputes that can't be settled on a day-to-day basis.

This is not the place for every petty squabble, but if Bobby keeps going into Billy's room and taking his comic books, and if you've tried talking to Bobby, and even grounding him, to no avail, Family Council Meetings are a place to bring up the problem and try to settle it.

- Does Bobby think he has justification?
- Does Annette have a solution, as a child herself, that you as an adult might not have thought of?
- Is this an opportunity for a general discussion of respecting other people's rights and property?

The Council is the appropriate place for discussions of such subjects as allowances, too. Is it time for a raise all across the board? Or maybe just for Annette? Since Mom went back to work, is Annette doing appreciably more cooking and other chores? If she's carrying a greater burden, maybe it's time for an allowance raise for her.

You, as parents, should recognize that she deserves the raise *before* she has to ask; the Council is a good place to award it to her, when the other kids are listening. They'll get the message: Pitch in and take on more chores, and it won't go unappreciated. But if you *don't* bring it up first, the Council Meeting is a good place for Annette to make the request herself: "Hey, I'm doing a lot more around the house since Mom went back to work. How about a bigger allowance?"

Is it time to reassign chores? As the kids get older, giving them more chores is appropriate. Use the Council Meetings to make new assignments. And if the kids want to trade chores, Council is a good place for them to make such arrangements... with your approval.

Do you have Billy assigned to putting away dishes and Bobby to raking leaves? Did Bobby used to be too short to reach the cabinets? Maybe he's tall enough to put the dishes away now. Does Billy have lots of homework these days? Maybe he could trade with Bobby, who now rakes leaves on weekends or does some other chore the timing of which is better for Billy.

Do the kids have specific requests about other matters, ranging from menu-planning to TV rules? Now's the time to bring them up. How about general rules? "I don't know why you won't let me walk to Ronnie's house alone! Ronnie's mom lets him walk over here alone!"

Is there a mother alive who doesn't hate the words "So-and-so's mom lets *him* do it!" or "All the other kids do it." Nine times out of ten, the argument is baseless. You have your rules, they're well grounded, and you don't care what other moms do... you know what's best for your kids.

But there's that tenth time. Are you holding your kids back, not recognizing that they're older and ready for some next step? Ready to cross streets alone, or stay out playing after dark, or have a co-ed party, or wear makeup? Are you trying to keep your babies as babies a little too long, or being a nervous mom, or just genuinely not realizing they're old enough to move up a notch in privileges?

The Family Council Meeting is a good place for them to bring up requests for increased privileges and freedom. *This doesn't mean you have to give in to every request...* or *any* request... all you have to do is listen open-mindedly.

What about bedtimes? That's another privilege that's suitable for discussing at meetings. If Bobby's bedtime has been 8:30 for two years, maybe he *is* ready to stay up till 9:00. Discuss it in Council.

How about family vacations—are you planning to all go away over Christmas vacation, or a week or two in the summer? Maybe the trip is to visit Grandma, and there's no room for debate. But if you've been vacillating between a trip to the shore and one to the mountains, or a trip to Disney World or a ranch, let the kids have some voice in the matter.

That's not to say you have to abide by their wishes. Ultimately, other factors may have the last word in your decision, such as cost, or whether a seaside motel or mountain cabin has room for you on the week in question. But if all other factors are equal, or if there's still some room for decision-making, at least give the kids a chance to put their two cents' worth in.

Does Billy need homework help that you can't give him? Is the elementary school teaching the kids French this year, and you don't know a single word of the language? Elicit help from Annette, who's studying first-year French in high school. (If long-term help is needed here, and you think it's appropriate, you could consider paying her for tutoring.)

Not every little problem in a family is fodder for Family Council Meetings, but many grievances and requests—on your part as well as the kids'—are best brought up in such a forum. And sometimes one of the other kids will have the best solution.

Democracy works—as long as the kids remember you two are still the copresidents!

Creative Family-Oriented Thinking

Materials needed: none

If yours is a family that has Family Council Meetings, or something similar, there are other topics that are suitable for Council discussions along with allowance requests, disciplinary actions, and chore assignments. If you don't have a Family Council, these topics are still worth round-table discussions.

These could take place over dinner, after dinner, at times when there's nothing on TV and the kids are complaining they're bo-o-o-ored, or just at a time you feel you want to set aside especially for such discussions.

The topics I have in mind run along the lines of How This Family Could Be Improved. Naturally the kids are going to come up with, "fewer chores," "higher allowance," "later bed-time," and such.

Nine times out of ten, you'll say "Nice try," and vote them down, but occasionally a request such as "higher allowance" will be valid. Kids are entitled to "raises" too, whether based on number of years since last raise in allowance, increased chore responsibility, or just cost-of-living increases. (Don't laugh—prices of candy, comic books, and other such "necessities" go up when everything else goes up.)

But unless you feel they have a valid request, try to steer them away from "less study time" and "fewer chores," and into more constructive thinking. How *could* your family be improved?

- Should you be spending more time talking with the kids?
- Should you all be doing more active things together? (Presumably you're a family that does get involved in family projects, or you wouldn't have bought this book.)
- Do the kids need to do more to keep common areas clean?
- Do the kids need more praise and encouragement for positive accomplishments (more "carrot" and less "stick")?
- Do the kids want to take lessons in instruments, tap dancing, singing, gymnastics, or martial arts, while you've been denying the requests on the assumption it's just a passing phase?
- Conversely, do you have them scheduled for a different

lesson or Scouts or some other activity every afternoon, giving them no free time to just be kids?
• Are the kids grossly inconsiderate of each other's feelings?

Just how could this family be improved?
Talk it out.

"Top Ten" Lists

Materials needed: pen or pencil and paper

If the kind of problem-solving discussed in Creative Family-Oriented Thinking, above, isn't what your kids are good at, another way to come up with constructive suggestions for improving your family is the Top Ten list. Borrow a leaf from Letterman and have the kids each come up with a list...while you come up with one, too.

In fact, you want *two* lists each: Top Ten Good Things About This Family and Top Ten Things About This Family That Need Changing. If the kids can't think of ways to actually improve the family (see above), they can usually think of what's wrong with it...at least in their estimation.

Some of the items on their list are going to be same-old complaints: too many chores, too strict rules against junk food or against too much TV-watching. Some are going to be standard sibling sniping: older sisters who don't respect privacy, younger brothers who have to tag along everywhere and get to be a pain. But mixed in with those, there's bound to be a valid criticism or two: Dad's always too busy to play football or catch, Mom favors one brother over another, Mom and Dad don't include the kids enough in the planning stage when making decisions that involve the whole family.

Consider each criticism seriously, even the ones that seem frivolous or manipulative. Are you sure you're not giving the kids too many chores or too little allowance? If they say you don't appreciate what they do around the house, are you sure you're not taking them for granted, or failing to praise them when praise is due? We all like to hear "Good job!" at the end of some task, and if the work merits praise, praise should be given.

If the complaint is that you're always too busy to spend time with the kids, are you taking on too much outside the family? Is there a corner you could cut to eke out a little more time for them?

If the complaint is about a sibling, discuss it as a group now.

You'll have made a "Good" and "Bad" list, too. It's only fair for you to air your grievances, and for the kids to hear them.

And then, when you're through taking apart the Top Ten...Change lists and discussing which items have merit and how the problems can be addressed, it's time for the other lists. The "Good" lists. Now here's a chance to remind yourselves that this family isn't so bad after all. What are the best things about this family? Read them out loud and proud. Resolve to build on your strengths, to make that which is good even better. And take pride in yourselves as a family unit.

Now there's one more set of lists you want to write: "Top Ten Good Things About _____"—one for each member of the family. Do your kids always grouse about each other? Do they complain that you're out-of-date in your thinking, too strict, too restrictive? But what about everyone's *good* points? Now's the time to get everyone thinking about the positive side.

Write those lists. If you think "Top Ten" is asking too much, make it "Top Five," but get the kids to focus on each other's—and your—good points. Get them to recognize the best of everyone. Then read *those* lists aloud, and build up your family pride.

8

Just For Fun

Family Talent Night

Materials needed: depends on which talents your family is showcasing—may require instruments, taped or recorded music, ballet or tap shoes, or?

Monica's been faithfully going to ballet lessons for months now, but her recital isn't till May, and she'd love to show off her newfound abilities before that. Yet, on the other hand, she's nervous about getting up in front of a whole audience full of strangers in May and dancing.

Bobby's a natural-born ham. He's been studying guitar for two years, but he takes private lessons, so there isn't any recital for him to show off at.

Dad's an accomplished pianist...a bit rusty but good. And Mom sings in an untrained but sweet, clear voice.

What this family needs is a Family Talent Night. This can be a regular practice (say, the first Sunday evening of every month), a once-in-a-while event, or a one-shot deal. Any way you do it, it's a chance for the kids to show off, a chance for them to get used to performing in front of an audience, a chance for them to properly recognize that their parents have more abilities than those of working at a job or running a household, and a chance for them to appreciate each other.

You can make Family Talent Night an occasion when you simply entertain each other or you can invite relatives who live nearby; you can even let the kids invite their friends. If the kids

183

have more than one talent or ability, let them show them *all* off. If, besides the fact that Seth plays a mean saxophone now that he's taking lessons, he also has a deft hand at card tricks, let him perform both music *and* magic.

The talents the kids showcase don't have to be only those for which they've been taking lessons. Formal training and proficiency are not the criteria here—ability and enjoyment are. If your child's proficiency at his or her favorite performance art is somewhat lacking, encourage him or her anyhow. Even Michael Jackson, Beverly Sills, and Rudolf Nureyev were undoubtedly in need of improvement when each of them first opened a mouth or pointed a leg. If you have a child who isn't taking lessons and has no special talent for performing, let him or her be the show's M.C.

If the kids get good at it, and really get into performing, consider taking the "act" to local nursing homes. Those folks need all the company and all the cheering up they can get. The kids can get their kicks showing off and do a good deed at the same time. It's a win-win situation: Everybody gets something good out of the deal, and what could be better than that?!

Customized Family Board Games

Materials needed: one or more commercial board games
that lend themselves to customization as explained below
(examples include Monopoly, Careers, and Parcheesi),
paper, pen, paste or glue or tape

Imagine if, instead of vying to buy Boardwalk, you and your family were contending for the rights to... *your* street! Suppose Grandma's street was the other purple-coded street, prized for its hotel-rental value, instead of Park Place.

It can be done.

In fact, the names of *all* the streets in Monopoly can be changed to those of streets in your town. All it takes is pen, paper, and glue or paste or tape. And other board games can be similarly altered, reflecting the names of family members, their career choices, or their personal habits.

Mom's real boss's name can pop up in Payday. Career paths in Careers can reflect family members' real-life goals: rock 'n' roll star, nuclear physicist, owner of a llama ranch, writer of books on fly-fishing, hockey player.... Why not? It makes the game more meaningful for the members of your family.

By altering the appropriate areas of a commercial board game, everyone in the family is made aware of those things that are unique to this group of people and make them a family; memories, facts, plans, names, and expectations all get mirrored in the personalization of these games.

There are some guidelines to customizing:

• Customizing with removable transparent tape will allow you to change what you've customized, if Eileen's career choice or Dad's boss's name changes, or even if you move and want the street names on your customized Monopoly board to reflect the streets in your new town. (Though what a nice reminder of your old home it will be to keep playing Monopoly with the old names.)

- It's generally better if you don't change the actual rules of the game. There's a complex interrelationship of the parts of successful game rules that can be thrown seriously out of kilter if fundamental aspects of play are altered.
- The games that most easily lend themselves to customization are those that in some way deal with either personalities of players, people's names, or place names. There's not a whole lot you can do with checkers or Sorry, for instance. But in Parcheesi, you can fill the stops with family-related rewards and punishments. ("Andrea spills her milk at dinner; lose one turn to clean up." "Kim gets new tennis shoes; sprint ahead three paces.")

Yet none of the above is etched in stone. There *are* ways to customize checkers *and* change the rules, for instance, for those who aren't purists. One such is to institute a rule that a checker reaching the far side of the board is not automatically made a king; the player must first answer a family trivia question, written on an index card. Reaching the far row merely entitles you to answer the question; you must get the answer correct before your checker can be crowned. And if you don't get the answer right, you have to wait another turn, answer another question, and hope you're right this time.

Examples of questions:

- What was the date of Mom and Dad's wedding?
- Where were Mom and Dad married?
- What was Mom's major in college?

When everyone knows all the answers to all the questions by heart, put those questions aside for a month-long rest and substitute a new deck of questions.

And, if you run out of reasonable questions about the immediate family, start on questions about other close relatives:

- When is Aunt Syl's birthday?
- What business is Uncle Lenny in?
- Name three lawyers in the family.
- What rank did Grandpa rise to in the army?

In fact, if you can think of enough family trivia questions, you can make up a whole game out of it. Take any board game you have around the house that includes a board one moves around on from a starting point to a finishing point, playing pieces representing the players, and one die for tossing. (Or use a board game with the appropriate path to move around and a spinner that goes from one to six. Or use a board game with the appropriate path and a die or spinner from another game.)

Now write, on individual index cards, as many family trivia questions, and the right answers, as you can think of. Everyone should contribute to the index cards, not just the parents. The kids need a chance to think of their own questions:

- Who was Karen's first-grade teacher?
- Name Tim's favorite camp counsellor.
- What was the class song at Thea's elementary-school graduation?

Each player rolls the die. The highest roller goes first, and play proceeds clockwise around the table from there. The first player now rolls the die or spins the spinner. The player to his or her left takes the top card of the trivia card pile and reads the question aloud. If the player whose turn it is gives the right answer, he or she advances a number of spaces equivalent to the number that came up on the die or spinner. If the answer is wrong, he or she has to stay put till the next turn. (*Variation:* S/he has to move backward that number of spaces.)

The first player to move completely around the board is the winner. (*Note:* It is not necessary to roll the exact number needed to cross the finish line. If you need to move two spaces and roll a four, you can still advance across the finish line if you answer the question correctly.)

Snow Paintings

Materials needed: four spray bottles, four small containers of food coloring (one each red, blue, yellow, green), water

Want to have fun in the snow... fun that's less ordinary than throwing snowballs or making snowmen, snow forts, and castles, and won't get you all wet the way lying down to make "snow angels" will? How about creating a painting with snow as your canvas and food coloring as your medium?

The whole family can work together on one painting, or you can divide the yard into large rectangles, one for each family member, so that each has his or her own area to work in. If you do divide up the yard, be sure you leave a walkway on all sides of each rectangle so that the artists have room to walk without tramping on their own or other family members' canvases.

How large an area each artist gets will be determined by how large a yard you have to divide up, but in all cases, be sure you don't make the area so large that the artist can't reach it from one side or another.

Now fill the spray bottles with water, adding about five drops of food coloring to each bottle—more if it's a large bottle or you're looking for a more intense color, less if it's a small bottle or you're looking for a more muted color.

You can draw landscapes, portraits, or abstract art. In fact, you can draw a beach scene, complete with palm trees, if you want to remind yourself that warmer days are somewhere ahead. Let each artist have a turn with each color.

If there are more than four of you in the family, and if your kids are too young to be patient, you can fill more bottles so no one has to wait—though they still may have to wait for a specific color. ("I get the green next!" "No, I do!" "Mommmmmm, he's hogging the yellow!")

Oh, well...nobody said this activity was totally squabble-free in anything larger than a one-child family, but if dissension does break out in the ranks, the air can always be cleared with a good old-fashioned snowball fight—the materials are right at hand and don't cost a cent.

Rebuses and Similar Puzzles

Materials needed: paper and pens or pencils

Most kids are familiar with rebuses, in which a letter or picture is made to stand for a whole word. A picture of a bee represents the word *be*, and a picture of an eye represents the word *I*. The numeral 4 stands for *for* (or even *fore*), and a 2 is used for *to* or *too*. A picture of a bee, a "plus" symbol ($+$) and the numeral 4 together spell out "before." $4+2+N+8$ means "fortunate." I M $4+2+N+8$ 2 NO U reads "I am fortunate to know you." Whole spelled-out words are used where necessary, but as sparingly as possible.

One of the better-known rebuses, involving no pictures at all, is:

YY U R
YY U B
I C U R
YY 4 ME

and translates:

Too wise you are.
Too wise you be.
I see you are
Too wise for me.

A related type of puzzle is that in which the placement of words gives a clue to their intended meanings. Perhaps the most famous example is that of an alleged address on an envelope that, in three words, is supposed to spell out a whole address. Of course, since the days when this one was invented, it is no longer believable that an envelope would be delivered without a street address on it, but it still makes for a good puzzle:

WOOD
JOHN
MASS.

The solution to this one is:

John Underwood
Andover, Massachusetts
(John, *under* Wood *and over* Massachusetts.)

So get your kids busy making up their own rebuses and similar puzzles. When they've devised the puzzles, let everyone have a look at everyone else's—this includes you parents, too—and try to solve them all. (You may be surprised to find that your kids solve them at least as quickly as you do, if not faster.)

Telephone Words

Materials needed: pen or pencil and paper, telephone

What's your telephone number? Mine's WOW A LOG. Perhaps yours is EAT FISH; if your phone number happens to be 328-3474, it converts to EAT FISH when you match the numerals with the letters that appear with them. If your number is 465-3464, let's hope your favorite sport is GOLFING, because that's what your numbers spell out.

Stuck for a way to kill half an hour? Get your kids to figure out words for numbers they call often. Start with your own number. Numbers with ones or zeros in them won't convert to words, since there are no letters that match up to the 1 or 0 on a telephone dial, but any other phone number is fair game for conversion to a word or phrase.

The numeral 2 is associated with A, B, and C on the phone dial. The 3 is D, E, and F. And so on. By playing around with all possible letter combinations, your kids (and you) may come up with some clever, funny, or memorably ridiculous words or phrases that your phone number "translates" to.

When you're through working over your own phone number, try the same thing with other numbers familiar to your family—your best friend, your kids' friends, Grandma, the school, the library, Aunt Mae, your office.

It may even be easier for the kids to memorize a word than a seven-digit number, and if turning your office number into a word helps them remember how to reach you in an emergency, you've just turned a fun game into a useful tool indeed.

Limericks

Materials needed: pen and paper

Ever since Edward Lear gave us the limerick, in the middle of the nineteenth century, this jocular form of poetry has been one of the more popular kinds of English verse. Though frequently noted for being bawdy or ribald, not all limericks are off-color. One popular limerick goes:

> The lim'rick packs laughs astronomical,
> But often the joke's anatomical.
> The good ones I've seen
> Are so seldom clean
> And the clean ones are so seldom comical.

Yet the reality is that a good *clean* laugh can often be found in a limerick... especially if the subject of the verse is a member of your family. And a limerick is an easy verse form to write. You're probably familiar with the format already; if not, the example above gives you a fair idea of the structure and meter, though the meter has been tampered with slightly. Though minor variations in the meter are permissible, the structure is basically:

> Dah-DAH-dah-dah-DAH-dah-dah-DAH.
> Dah-DAH-dah-dah-DAH-dah-dah-DAH.
> Dah-DAH-dah-dah-DAH.
> Dah-DAH-dah-dah-DAH.
> Dah-DAH-dah-dah-DAH-dah-dah-DAH.

With this knowledge, all the members of your family can set about writing limericks. Though some will no doubt be about events or people at school and elsewhere, family members will probably be the targets in most cases. And that's all right—how much better for brother to get out his aggressions against sister in verse form than by pinching her, or putting the family's goldfish down her back. (But if he's already done the goldfish bit, why not commemorate it in a limerick!)

The lines may be awkward and the syntax tortured, but soon brother will come up with this about his sister, or something of its ilk:

> There once was a girl name of Jane
> Whose face was so awfully plain
> That it frightened her mother
> And freaked out her brother
> And gave all her schoolmates great pain.

She, of course, will respond with something along the lines of:

> There once was a brother named Jay
> Who did nothing all day but just play.
> This terrible lad
> Was so awfully bad
> That his family wished he'd go away.

OK, neither of the above examples is going to win a Pulitzer, and neither will the ones your own kids come up with, but they'll sure be fun (and they'll work out those hostilities in a socially acceptable fashion).

A few pointers: Though many limericks begin "There once was," it isn't necessary to start that way. If you do, it can be, "There once was a fellow named Jay," "There once was a young boy named Jay," "There once was a brother named Jay," or some other variation. If you're writing one about a fellow with a three-syllable name, you can still do something like, "A guy named Orestes was awful," "Orestes, a nerd, was so mean," etc. Internal rhyme aids the limerick, though it isn't crucial to the form. As an example:

A sister named Jane was a pain,
Very plain, loud, and born without brain.
In a fit of good taste
Mom re-named Jane as "waste,"
And plain Jane went right down the drain.

But please don't assume that all family limerick-writing
needs to consist of an exchange of insults. What of siblings who
get along exceptionally well? What of "only" children? And
anyhow, why ignore all those other good targets? There are
teachers, even people in the news worth poking fun at; there are
events in the kids' lives—and yours—that merit retelling in
limerick form. And there are just-for-fun limericks that skewer
no one, commemorate nothing, but just have fun with the
printed word.

Older kids can make up literate limericks, or those involving
wordplay. The following is an example of both:

There once was a poet named Donne
Who had some strange notions of fonne.
Like his friend Butler Yeats
He did not go on deats
And his "girl" was a Carmelite nonne.

Once the kids get the hang of how to construct a basic
limerick, there are various types of fun the family can have
together beyond just writing limericks independently:

• Family members sit in a circle, each with a piece of
  paper and a pen. Each writes the first line of a limerick,
  then passes the paper to the person on the left. Now
  each person has in front of him or her someone else's first
  line, for which each is required to write a second line
  before passing the paper again to the left. Then each has
  to write a third line (on yet a different limerick), and so
  on, till each piece of paper has been through five pairs of

hands (which will include some of the same hands twice, unless there are five or more people in the family).

• Again, each family member has a paper and pen in front of him or her, but this time one person comes up with a first line, and each family member has to construct, without peeking at his or her neighbor, a limerick beginning with that line. At the end, the various versions are compared, with each person reading his or hers aloud. Not only is it going to be interesting to hear the variety of rhymes likely to be chosen, but also the offbeat directions in which different people take the same opening.

The limerick may not be the definition of high art, but it's likely to provide high times for any family that gets a kick out of playing around with words and sounds.

Captions Outrageous

Materials needed: old photos that you don't want (of people), scissors, typing paper, pencils, glue or paste

Here's a fun way to use up some of those pictures you took that just didn't come out right.

• Does Aunt Edna, positioned in front of a young maple, appear to have a thin tree growing out of her head?
• Was Mom squinting or frowning or yawning just when the shutter clicked?
• Does Grandpa's expression suggest there was too much

pepper in the chili he ate before you got that shot?
- Did Spot ruin the picture of Jeff by lifting his leg just when the camera went off?

You needn't throw those pictures out. I've got a creative way for the family to use them. This activity, a distant "cousin" to Comical Books (see page 63), involves melding pictures and words for a comical effect. And everyone—parents and kids alike—can get into the act if they want to.

Cut comic-strip-style "balloons" out of the typing paper, and paste a balloon onto each of the discarded pictures. You're going to be writing words in the balloons, so each one should be positioned to indicate that the person in each picture is speaking. In each balloon, write a suitably funny quotation.

Alternative: If the picture seems better suited to editorial comment than to an outrageous quotation, skip the balloon and paste a strip of paper along the top or bottom of the picture, writing the comment in there.

Divide the photos evenly among family members, letting everyone have a chance at coming up with outrageous captions. Then pass the pictures around the table, so everyone can have a good laugh.

If someone else at the table thinks of a marvelously better caption for a picture than the one it now carries, and family consensus favors the change, change it. Since the captions have been written in pencil, you can always erase the original caption and replace it with the improved version.

The best of the captioned photos can even find their way to the kitchen bulletin board, fridge door, or other suitable spot.

Cow Bingo

Materials needed: crayons, Cow Bingo Cards
(see below)

Cow Bingo is a game designed to keep kids occupied during
a car trip—or conceivably a train trip. You need to prepare for
the game ahead of time. For each child in the car, you need one
card (two or more if you're going to play two or more games).
Draw a grid five boxes across by five boxes up and down in
standard Bingo fashion, except that you needn't letter in
BINGO above the top of the columns. The central square is
marked FREE. In the others, instead of the usual Bingo
numbers, write items that you're likely to pass as you drive.

Don't write all the same items on every card, though a fair
amount of duplication is expected. Where there is duplication,
don't write all the items in the same places on each card. That
is, if *red barn* appears in the second space of the third row on
one card, it might appear in the fourth space of the fifth row on
another card.

Which items you'll choose to fill in the squares will depend
on where you're going to be driving... along small-town roads,
a superhighway, through farmland, or on the roads of a busy city.
Some items you might use to fill in the squares, depending on
the type of driving you'll be doing, are *brown cow, black dog,*
very large dog, soda billboard, schoolbus, yellow tractor, blue
Buick, red convertible, fire hydrant, drugstore, firehouse,
school, gas station, or *cemetery.*

Each child, on spotting one of the items on his or her card,
yells it out. The *first* child to yell an item out gets credit for it,
and gets to cross it off his or her card with a crayon slash. The
other kids don't get credit for that particular horse, blinking

yellow light, hospital, or whatever. When a child has completed a full line—vertically, horizontally, or diagonally—he or she yells "Bingo!" and is declared a winner.

But the game isn't over yet.

Keep going in the same manner, till one child gets the whole card marked out. Now *she or he* yells "Bingo!"—it may be the same child again, or another one—and is declared a winner, too.

Now the game is over; but you can pass out more cards, now or an hour from now, and play again. If you wish, a little prize (such as a small box of raisins or an inexpensive toy) can be awarded to each winner, but there's nothing wrong with winning for the sheer fun of being triumphant, no prizes needed.

Interfamily Competitions

Materials needed: depends on the types of games you choose to play

Politicians, statesmen, and, .yes, dictators down through the ages have known that one way to foster civic or national pride is to stir up a spirit of "us against them." Whether it's "We have a cleaner city" or "Our country is the greatest," pitting one group against another generally serves to stir up a feeling of pride, community, and togetherness among the citizens of a given locality.

This same pride of citizenship applies to families, too. So why not follow the politicans' example—in a minor key—and knit your family tighter together by engaging in a very good-natured competition with one or more other families?

The most logical format for this competition is a field day of athletics and games. It can be an informal and quite mild competition between you and one other family, consisting of just a few games after a picnic feast on the first warm day of spring. Or you can get more gung-ho, organize any number of families, really work up a long list of events to be competed in, and possibly even award homemade trophies to the team that wins the greatest number of events.

You can invite one other family to join you at the local park— or even in your back yard, if it's spacious enough—eat a picnic lunch, talk for a little while as lunch settles, and then engage in such events as a tug of war, pitting one family against the other, relay races, with each family being one team, and whatever other competitions you feel are appropriate. Sack races, three-legged races, and wheelbarrow races are all good possibilities for events at your interfamily competition.

If yours is a particularly "green" family, you might also want to include a garbage-pick-up competition. Both families go around the park collecting paper plates, aluminum cans, and other refuse left behind by other careless picnickers. The family that collects the most trash wins that event. Other less traditional events are also possible... really, the only limits are your imagination and practicality.

It's best, particularly for the traditional games, if you compete against one or more families that are constituted similarly to yours. A family of one parent and one child can't compete fairly against a family of two parents and two kids. A family of two parents, a toddler, and a five-year-old can't compete fairly against a family of two parents and three teenagers. But surely you know at least one other family whose composition is similar to your family's.

As your son and his opponent from the other family hop backward toward the finish line, Kate, who was fighting nastily with her brother just this morning, will be standing there loudly cheering him on. As Kate and her counterpart on the other team race toward the finish line while carrying potatoes on spoons, Max will be cheering on the sister he was tormenting three hours ago.

Go, Family!

Puppet Theater

Materials needed:

For the "stage": *either a sheet draped over the dining room table, or a sheet draped over a stack of milk cartons, or an actual puppet theater built by someone in the family who's a handy carpenter*

For sock puppets: *white or pale socks, cotton or any other suitable stuffing, paint, buttons, yarn or crepe paper, glue, thin strip of cardboard, scissors*

For spool puppets: *empty thread spool, paint, yarn or crepe paper, glue, scissors, small stick or pencil*

It's possible to buy a complete puppet theater—stage, puppets, even simple backdrops—if you want. It's also expensive. If your kids are into puppetry but not crafts, a store-bought puppet theatre, complete with puppets, may be the way to go. But if they're typical of most kids, they'll get as much pleasure out of creating the puppets as out of putting on the show. And puppets made of socks or spools, while not as elaborate as papier-mâché or other kinds of puppets, are easy and quick to make, and quite inexpensive.

Let's deal with the theater, first. The most rudimentary puppet theater can be made at simply by draping a sheet across a table, so the audience can't see the puppeteers. The sheet drapes down to the floor on one long side of the table, and the puppeteers crouch or kneel behind the other long side.

A similar effect can be achieved by stacking milk cartons and draping a sheet over them. Now that you can buy plastic pseudo–milk cartons in the store, more people than before have these cartons in their home.

Or if someone in the family is handy with carpentry, he or she can build a puppet stage.

Two of the simplest kinds of puppets to create are sock puppets and spool puppets. For each spool puppet you need one empty thread spool. Paint the eyes, nose, mouth, and possibly ears. Create the hair by cutting either crepe paper or yarn, then gluing it to the top of the spool. A pencil stuck in the bottom of the spool manipulates the puppet. You'll need to sharpen the pencil first, to make it fit. Then you may want to break off the lead point, for safety's sake, if you have young kids. Finally, you can glue the pencil into the hole for added security; otherwise, if the puppet takes a bow, it could lose its head.

You can color in a blush on the puppet's cheeks, or add any other touches you'd like, but essentially your puppet is now finished. Spool puppets don't have arms or clothing. They don't have movable parts. They're very basic.

Sock puppets are created out of light-colored socks. (Even if you want to depict an African-American, light-colored socks are recommended so the features are easily visible. Just use a light tan instead of white.)

Stuff the sock with cotton, or any other suitable soft material you have. (There are a number of options available at crafts stores, or if you happen to be discarding a foam rubber pillow, you can cut up the foam rubber to stuff the sock with.)

• The eyes can be painted on, or you can sew buttons on.

- Eyebrows (painted on, or made of glued-on crepe paper) are optional, as are painted-on lashes.
- The mouth should be painted.
- The nose can be painted or can be a small pink button.
- The hair, again as with the spool puppets, can be made from either yarn or crepe paper, glued on.

A thin band of cardboard, wrapped around the sock below the face and glued together, constricts the sock and forms a neck while holding the cotton in place. It should be wide enough for the puppeteer's index finger, and not much wider. Cut a hole on either side of the sock just below the neckband. The puppeteer's thumb and middle finger will stick out of these holes, serving as the puppet's arms.

If you wish, you can sew two or three buttons in a line downward from the neck, suggesting clothes, but this isn't necessary.

Each puppeteer can operate two puppets at a time. So for a two-character show, you only need one puppeteer. For a three- or four-character show, you need two puppeteers (unless no more than two puppets are ever on stage at one time), and so on.

What's your show going to be about? Of course, you can wing it, ad-libbing a conversation, perhaps even singing (and leading the audience in a sing-along). But it's generally more fun to put on an actual show that tells a story.

You can act out a famous fairy tale or other well-known story, such as Cinderella or Little Red Riding Hood. If you do, you can work from a script or ad-lib it. Most kids know these stories by heart, and a script isn't an absolute essential. But it never hurts, and it avoids lots of backstage whispering of the type, "No! You don't come in the door till after I've said, 'Is there no one in the land this slipper fits?'"

Even better, you can write your own play, an original story.

Whether the puppeteers will write their own story, make the puppets, and put on the show, or whether different members of the family will undertake the various aspects of the production depends on how many people there are in the family and what their areas of interest and ability are.

One way to involve the whole family is a division of responsibility such as this:

- An older child builds a theater.
- The two younger kids make the puppets.
- Mom and a younger child write the show.
- Dad and another younger child put on the show.

Or Mom and Dad can simply be the audience. The audience is very important too...without one, there's no one to put on a show for. Though, of course, you can always put the show on for other kids or families in the neighborhood.

If the kids really get into puppetry, and it doesn't seem to be a passing phase, you might want to spring for fancy equipment. With assorted store-bought puppets and/or a fancy stage, the kids might be inspired to put on even grander shows, larger in concept. But on the other hand, they'd lose the fun of creating the puppets themselves...though they would still have the pleasure of writing the shows and performing them.

In the immortal words of Judy Garland and Mickey Rooney, "Hey kids...let's put on a show!"

Hot and Cold

Materials needed: one small object to hide

This game's been around for generations, maybe even centuries, but it seems to be played less now than in times past.

With the sophisticated amusements that are around today to occupy kids, too many parents forget the simple entertainments, or they doubt these basic games' ability to hold a child's interest.

Well, the little ones will still be amused by hiding-and-finding games, especially if there's a reward for the finder, though successfully finding the hidden object is usually reward enough.

In Hot and Cold, clues are given... you probably remember from your own childhood. A small object—a marble, a coin, a piece of paper, a small piece of candy—is hidden somewhere in a room. The seeker scouts all over, with clues from the hider as to whether the seeker is getting closer to the hidden object or farther away:

- "You're cold" means you're far away from it.
- "You're getting warmer" means you're getting nearer to it.
- "You're hot!" means you're very near it.

The pure joy of triumphant success is enough of a reward in most cases. If you add an actual treat, so much the better. Instead of hiding a marble or a penny or such, then taking it back when the seeker finds it, you can hide a quarter or a small candy bar, for the seeker to keep if she or he can find it. Or you can hide a piece of paper or something "redeemable" for a larger prize once it's found.

For a switch, let the kids hide something and give *you* clues as to whether you're "hot" or "cold" as you do the searching.

9

Miscellaneous Projects

Family Bike Hike

Materials needed: bike for each family member, helmets, map of your area, perhaps a picnic lunch

Most adults would be surprised to learn at how early an age kids are able (and delighted) to participate in long bike rides and the adventure of a family bike hike. I'm not talking about cycling from Minneapolis to Phoenix, though these longer-distance local outings will season the kids for cross-country tours, should that be your thing, and will give you a chance to see if it's their thing, too.

The bike hike should start with a plan. Yes, it's fun to just set out and cycle wherever your whim takes you, exploring unfamiliar roads or previously unexplored bike paths in the local park. But there's much to be said for planning ahead, knowing:

- Where you're going (and how to get back)
- That there definitely are roads to take that aren't too busy
- Where there's a place to stop and enjoy the picnic lunch you've packed (spread out the burden, putting a little in each biker's backpack or bike basket)

As you gather around the map, planning out your trip, the kids will familiarize themselves with maps and how to read them, and they will get to know your area better than they do now.

Keep your early expeditions modest in scope. You need to be sure the kids' legs and attention spans are up to the task at hand. If the trip proves exhausting or boring to one of the kids, nobody's going to have a good time. Your first trip should be to a reasonably nearby destination, preferably one that offers something of interest, so the kids enjoy not only the trip but a tangible reward at the far end.

You could set out for:

- A city park
- A county park
- A particularly special playground
- A picnic ground
- A bird sanctuary
- A wildlife park
- A favorite relative's house

But don't take the kids on their first bike hike to visit fuzzy-minded, funny-smelling, odd Great-Aunt Jane, whom they hate going to see. It will only provide disincentive to future bike hikes. If your first destination is someone's home, make sure it's someone the kids *like* visiting.

If your kids are relatively young, a three- or four-mile limit in each direction is reasonable at first; soon, if the youngest is ten or more, they'll be cycling eight or ten miles without thinking about it, and then going even greater distances.

Since a bike hike takes you through the out-of-doors, other activities can be integrated into the day, such as leaf-collecting, shell-collecting (if you're headed to the beach), flower-preserving, or bird-watching. You can visit local historical sites and teach the kids a little about local history. (They'll have a leg up on their classmates when they study local history in school.)

If you happen to have a van, or a car with a bike rack, and if your family is small enough that the van or rack will accommodate all your bikes, you needn't even be bound by the limitation of what's reachable from your home. You can pile into the car, bikes and all, drive some distance, park, take out the bikes, and set out from there.

So pack a sandwich, grab your helmet, and hop aboard!

Weekly Walk

Materials needed: none

There are family projects that are complex, projects that are expensive, ones that require collecting a good deal of materials and doing a lot of planning and arranging... and then there are projects so simple, cheap (or free)—and yet enoyable and healthful—that it almost seems unnecessary to mention them in a book.

Yet I'll bet most people reading this don't go out for regular walks as a family.

Why not?

As is so often (and so ironically) the case, it's sometimes the simplest projects that are among the most-enjoyed activities, and among the most treasured memories in years to come. What could be simpler than taking a walk? And doctors say it's among the most healthful of exercises.

You've no time to go walking, you say? I'm not suggesting you go walking every day... just once a week. Are the kids watching an hour of TV a week? There's an hour that could be devoted to walking. You, too, have things you're doing that could be pushed aside, skipped, or otherwise moved around for *just one hour a week*. Come on, now...you know you could find an hour if you had something special you wanted to do.

Where you walk is entirely up to you and will have an effect on the nature of the walk you take. Do you live in the city, suburbs, or country? There are plenty of places to walk in your neighborhood, in any case...and if you own a car, you can pile in, drive a distance, and walk there—which isn't a bad idea in any event: It'll keep the kids from getting bored by seeing the same old scenery every time.

If you live in a city, why not combine your walks with architectural exploration, familiarizing the kids (and yourselves) with the different styles of architecture to be found in different neighborhoods around the city. Another option in the city is ethnic neighborhoods. Is there a Chinatown, Little Italy, or other ethnic enclave in your city or town? Why not combine the walk with a stop for lunch (or even dinner), so you can sample some ethnic goodies?

And if you live in a city, there's surely a park somewhere nearby. Explore it, familiarizing yourselves with the flowers and trees. Consider bringing along a little guidebook that identifies the different forms of flora, so you know just what kind of tree this is, what kind of flower that is.

If you're urban-dwellers (or even if you're not), you may want your walks some weeks to take place in a downtown environment, where window-shopping is the order of the day. There are usually enough kinds of stores in a downtown area that everyone can find something to daydream over in a window, whether it's clothes, appliances, fishing gear, toys, books, or electronics.

If you live in a city, travel around by car, bus, or subway and get to know different neighborhoods. Even in the suburbs, visiting different neighborhoods can be interesting. Or visit a nearby town and take your walk there, letting the kids see the similarities and differences between this town and your town.

Now's a great chance to sharpen their powers of observation and deduction. What can they tell you about this town, and how

it differs from your town, just by observing the houses or stores?
Are the streets cleaner? Are the houses bigger, the lawns
broader, the houses set back farther? Do the types of stores
found in the shopping district tell them something about the
people who live around here?

Walks can be great times to share observations of the sights
around you, or they may be occasions for retelling family
history. They can be a chance for kids to ask questions that have
been on their minds, or for you, the parents, to discuss the
weightier issues you hate to bring up when the TV is blaring in
the background, distracting them, the phone is ringing with yet
another call for them, homework is waiting, and the last of
daylight is tempting them to go out for just a half hour more.
Now's a great time for discussions of ethics, values discussions,
and other serious stuff that is best gotten into away from
distractions.

Or maybe you want your walks to be quiet times, times of
kicking pebbles, examining rocks and leaves, listening to birds,
and not saying much of anything, just enjoying being together
and soaking up the world around you firsthand, as opposed to
from nature specials on television.

Not that I'm knocking nature specials; TV has its good points,
and one of them is certainly being able to get a close-up view of
an Amazon rain forest while seated right in your living room.
But there's a time for that and a time for getting out in the real
world and examining a flower or a frog with your own eyes and
hands, hearing bird calls with your own ears and not through
the magic of enhanced stereo.

And speaking of bird songs, what about people's songs—if
you're walking in an unpopulated rural area, or a bustling, noisy
urban one, where no one will be disturbed by bursts of song,
why not all sing while you're walking.

But whether you use your weekly walks as a chance to study
urban architecture or the song of the whippoorwill, whether
you use it as a chance to sing or to discuss what careers your

high school kids are considering or what your first-grader's science project is, whether you're walking among skyscrapers or alongside cow pastures, or whether you're doing all these things on different weeks, walk regularly, walk together, make it a time of sharing, and you'll be creating a memory the kids will treasure for years to come, and getting them into a healthful habit now.

"Toys R Not Us" Day

Materials needed: Whatever is around the house or outdoors that is not a manufactured toy

What if a ray from outer space suddenly evaporated all manufactured toys? What would your kids *do*? With no electronic games, no boxed games, no teddy bears, no manufactured dollhouses, what would your kids do for fun?

Give them a chance to find out. They may surprise themselves with their ingenuity. There is a section on homemade games elsewhere in this book, but aside from those games, there are plenty of simple amusements that the kids can concoct. Turn a little one loose with a large spoon and a pot, and they'll soon be banging a homemade "drum." Pieces of cardboard can be crayoned and taped together for an impromptu dollhouse, with the dolls also cut out of cardboard, or paper.

Bolsters or pillows can be used to create an imaginary fort. A sheet draped over a bridge table makes a house or school. If you're not offended by the use of books for other than their intended purpose, structures can be created with (preferably hardbound) books—towers, castles, whole cities.

Kids can set pine cones on end outdoors, then see from what great distances they can knock them over with pebbles or stones. A stick or twig can be used to draw in the dirt...and what's drawn might be the board for a made-up game that will become a new family favorite. With a bit of imagination, twigs or large leaves can even substitute for dolls, cowboys, soldiers, or other figures.

A "no toys day" may be a once-in-a-lifetime occurrence in your family, or you could mandate it on a regular or semiregular basis. It makes the kids rely on their ingenuity and imagination, two "muscles" whose growth can get stunted with the easy availability of boxed and electronic games and the ever-present, attention-commanding television screen.

But it's never too late to liberate your kids...and to free their imaginations. Try it tomorrow—or today!

Raising Tropical Fish

Materials needed: see below for an itemization of equipment needed, all available at your local tropical fish outlet

If the kids want a pet but aren't ready for the responsibility of a cat or dog, or if you live in an apartment where cats and dogs aren't allowed—or even if you already have a cat, a dog, a gerbil, and a hamster—consider raising tropical fish. Tropicals are pretty, watching them is soothing (doctors say watching them

can actually lower some people's blood pressure), the responsibilities aren't as great as with a dog, yet your kids will still feel
pride of ownership.

True, you can't pet or cuddle a guppy, but then neither do
you have to take it for a walk two or three times a day, nor will it
chew electrical wires, claw your leg, have an "accident" on the
rug, swipe your sandwich when your back is turned, or wake up
all of you (and half the neighborhood) by barking at a car door
slamming outside at two in the morning.

Here's what you'll need to get started:

- A tank. You can start with a ten-gallon tank
- An air pump
- A filter
- Unless you keep your house quite warm year-round,
  you'll need a heater, and a thermometer. The
  temperature in the tank should be maintained at around
  75° or 80°F.
- You may also want a hood and light
- Food—and when the fish start having babies, you'll want
  special newborn food for the baby fish.
- Gravel is decorative, optional but usual
- Also recommended is a good, inexpensive book about
  raising tropical fish. There are any number; ask your fish
  dealer to recommend one.

The easiest tropicals to raise are the live-bearers (fish that
give birth to live young, rather than laying eggs). There are four
fish of this type:

- Molly
- Guppy
- Platy
- Swordtail, commonly called sword.

You can buy one, two, three, or all four types; they will live
together harmoniously. Egg layers are more difficult to raise,

though among them, the easiest are the betta and angel.

For kids who aren't ready to shoulder the responsibilities of owning a cat or dog, raising fish is a good way to ease into undertaking the responsibilities of pet ownership. And they— and you—will get oceans of enjoyment out of your tank of tropicals.

Special Events Pig

Materials needed: empty plastic one-gallon bleach bottle, paint or magic marker, pipe cleaner, possibly ice pick or awl, toothpicks, corks

A small but worthwhile ongoing family project that pays off in several ways is the creation of a Special Events Pig. This project brings the family together in the creation of the piggy bank itself, in accumulating the money, in family discussions of what treat is to be enjoyed with the money, and then in enjoying it. And as the set-aside cash in the belly of your homemade plastic porker grows before the eyes of your kids, they'll learn a valuable lesson about saving, even if they haven't been able to keep from raiding their personal piggy banks.

We're not talking Caribbean Cruise fund here, though I suppose that scale of project would be possible, too, over enough years and with parental help. But why think on such a grand and hard-to-reach scale? Pick a treat you don't often spring for out of your own pocket. It could be a night at the pizza parlor or a nicer restaurant that the kids enjoy, a day at the water-slide park, an edible orgy of triple-scoop banana splits, a visit to the miniature golf course, or any other treat... preferably one that the kids aren't likely to get out of you under normal circumstances.

The basis of the piggy bank is an empty plastic one-gallon bleach bottle. Transforming the bottle into the family's hungry porker is a simple matter. How much of the work you'll do yourself and how much the kids will depends on the ages of your children.

After rinsing the bleach bottle thoroughly, lay it on its side, noticing how it's now shaped sort of like a pig. Put the handle in a downward position, as if under the pig's chin. In the middle of what's now the pig's back, cut a slot about two inches long and one-eighth to one-quarter of an inch wide.

With paint or magic marker, draw eyes on your pig in the appropriate places. Draw nostrils on the nose (formerly the cap of the bottle). A twisted pipe cleaner serves as the pig's curly tail. Insert it into a hole in the appropriate site. You may need an ice pick or awl to punch the hole.

Toothpicks and corks make the bleach-bottle pig's four stubby legs. If your drawers aren't filled with old corks from wine, vinegar, or such, you can get them at a hobby and crafts store. Four toothpicks each get inserted into a cork at one end and into the bottle at the other end. The legs will hold the pig in place on the mantel, the family room window sill, or some other conspicuous spot where the family will be reminded of the need to fill it.

Just how to "feed" the pig is a question with several possible answers. Which method(s) you'll choose will depend in part on what the ages and resources of your kids are. Are they older kids with income from part-time jobs? Are they small ones with equally small allowances? Are they in-between, with some resources such as doing occasional odd jobs for neighbors, for example, raking leaves or shoveling snow?

- You can all agree that every child will put in a set amount every day, or every week.

- You can agree that each child will put in a different amount on some regular basis, the amount agreed upon by you and the child in accordance with his or her ability to pay.
- You can agree that each child will put in a certain percentage of whatever money he or she earns from odd jobs, comic books or lemonade sales, or other such enterprises.
- You can resolve that all money found outside on the street by any family member is to be contributed to the family pig.
- You can resolve that all money found under the couch cushions, on the floor, or wherever is to be contributed to the pig.
- You yourself can pay the pig a weekly allowance when you pay the kids their allowances.
- You can agree that every Saturday, or twice a week, whatever works for you, all pockets in the household are to be emptied of small change, with the coins being deposited in the pig.
- You can agree that, at the end of every day, every family member will empty his or her pockets of all pennies. It's a well-known fact that plastic pigs simply love to gorge on copper.
- I know of families that have "cuss banks." Every time a child utters language not acceptable to the parents, the child is fined a set amount. You can agree on something similar in your family. For each infraction of rules—not only inappropriate language, but *any* violation, or just certain violations previously agreed on—the offender is required to deposit a certain amount of money... in the Special Events Pig.

Any of these systems—or any combination of them—will work. You may even think of other means by which to fatten the porker. The important thing is to watch the money grow and, once you have an appreciable sum, to agree on what you're going to do with it.

This is a subject for family discussion, and one you may want to put to a vote. At the very least, the kids need to give some input.

- You may decide ahead of time that you're going to take your first "withdrawal" of funds from the pig on a certain date, and then decide what to do, based on how much is there.
- You may aim for a certain amount—say, $20—and count the money every Sunday night, having a family meeting when that amount is reached to decide how you're going to spend the money.
- You may set out with a specific goal in mind, counting the money weekly till you've reached the necessary amount for the treat, whether it's an outing to the amusement park or arcade, or a second Nintendo set to settle household squabbles over whose turn it is.

Though this isn't an elaborate family project, it does take on a life of its own and teaches a lesson as well...the value of saving. After the first time the pig is emptied and the money is put to good (and fun!) use, the kids will be even more eager to fill the pig again, knowing there's another family treat looming on the horizon.

This Family Is for the Birds!

Materials needed: books on birds

No matter where you live—East, West, North, South, city or town, farmhouse or tenth-floor apartment—your family can get a lot of enjoyment just looking out the window... at the birds. With nearly two thousand species of birds living and breeding in North America, you ought to be able to find a feathered friend *somewhere* near where your family lives. Thousands of amateur birdwatchers have identified more than fifty different kinds of birds just within ordinary suburban backyards, without the necessity of going anywhere special to spot them.

In the beginning, you needn't even engage in any formal study, trying to identify the birds you're watching. It's rewarding enough just to watch them, to notice details of the appearance and behavior of whatever birds happen to inhabit your part of the world. Even the most commonplace sparrows (there are more than thirty distinct species in this country) and street pigeons (look closely at the iridescence on their necks) take on a new and fascinating appearance to us once we start looking with an eye quickened by genuine interest.

Very soon after starting to pay attention to birds, however, the members of your family are sure to start having questions about what they're seeing. You need an expert to answer you, and fortunately those experts are as near as your bookstore or library.

Whichever book you choose, leaf through it and let some of the birds soak imperceptibly into your consciousness. One day, you'll catch yourself saying, "Gee, I think that's a junco," going to your bird book, and delightedly discovering you're correct.

Depending on how old your kids are, the interest in birds can progress into an opportunity for you to teach them more about natural science or biology, if you're knowledgeable (or can manage it with the aid of more library books). And if you don't know beans about the subject yourself, you can learn right along with the kids. Books (from the library or book store) will enlighten you on the birds' courtship and mating habits, how they nest, how they rear their young, what they eat... as much or as little as you feel your kids are going to be interested in and be able to comprehend.

As your family's knowledge about and interest in these fascinating creatures grows, you will find that you are going on more and more field trips and are participating in other entertaining and educational activities. A nearby museum or zoo might offer a chance to see other specimens of birds—stuffed or live—including more exotic species, and species that aren't found naturally in your part of the country.

Check with local ornithological societies to see what kinds of programs they offer the public—possibly slide shows, lectures, or actual birding field trips. Is there a bird sanctuary or wildlife sanctuary near your home? A family outing to such a place can be the source of some of your family's most treasured memories.

Once you begin to learn about birds, you'll find the amount of available information almost endless—and endlessly fascinating. Whatever level you get involved at, and whatever the ages of your kids, they—and you—will find much to absorb, involve, and entertain all of you together when you start watching birds.

Photo Collages

Materials needed: photos you don't want to keep in your album, scissors, paste, white cardboard or other background. (Optional: construction paper)

Here's another use for those "discard" photos that aren't all wrong, but aren't all right, either. If you've got a picture of Grandma Jean and Grandpa Phil, and she came out right but he didn't, and a picture of Cousin Ellie in which she's fine but the background is abominable, and a few other, similar shots, you've got the beginnings of a photo collage.

Carefully cut out the usable parts of the picture. If all of Cousin Ellie is fine, cut carefully around her whole body, snipping it from the bad background. If in a picture of Uncle Herb the face is fine but something went wrong with the body, cut out just the face and discard the rest.

When you have all the photos cut out, organize them on your background. The best background is a piece of white-coated cardboard, because it's fairly stiff and sturdy, and a bright, neutral color. If you haven't got a piece of white-coated cardboard available, you can use white paint over a piece of grey cardboard, use white typing paper and paste it to cardboard, or simply use white construction paper (a little sturdier than typing paper), as is.

You can also cut shapes out of construction paper, integrating them into the collage.

When you've got all the photos lined up the way you want, with one picture overlapping another or consruction paper cutouts overlapping pictures, start pasting. You can also, if you wish, cut out a brown "frame" of construction paper and paste it around the edges of the collage.

Mixed Media Photo-Drawings

Materials needed: photos that you'd otherwise toss out, scissors, construction paper or typing paper, crayons or paint or colored markers, paste or glue

Here's yet another use for photos from the discard pile.

• Got a picture of Aunt Judith in which the background

was fuzzy or Uncle Hal is standing next to her and got
caught mid-yawn?

• Got a picture of Uncle Ed in which his face reflects his
familiar grin but there's a big splotch of catsup on his
shirt that you didn't notice before you snapped the
shutter?

• Got a photo of Cousin Eileen that isn't out-and-out *bad*
but just didn't come out as good as the other three on
the same roll?

I've got a way for your kids to use them. Here's how:
Carefully cut around the good part of the picture. That means
either cutting around Aunt Judith's complete body and cutting
out Uncle Hal, or cutting around Uncle Ed's face and omitting
his body as well as the rest of the picture. (In the Cousin Eileen
picture you could go either way.)

Now paste the photo to a piece of typing or construction
paper, and draw whatever you want to go with it. If it's a picture
of Uncle Ed's face, you (that is, the kids, who are doing the
drawing) will probably want to draw in his body as well as some
kind of background... but in a minute we'll get to cases where
the body won't be drawn.

In the case of Aunt Judith's complete face and body, what
you'll draw in will be perhaps trees and flowers, perhaps her
dog... but it could also be an alien spacecraft, with its occu-
pants stepping out to tell her, "Take us to your leader," or a high
official from a mythical country placing a crown on her head,
making her ruler of Ruripotamia. Only your imagination will
limit just what gets drawn (or painted) around the photo or part
of photo you've snipped out.

Now what was that about *not* drawing in bodies? Well, there
are various imaginative things that can be done with three or
five heads. For one thing, they can be suspended up in the air,
with strings drawn down from them, making them appear to be
helium balloons, the strings gripped in the hand of a person.

(The person can be drawn or can be a photograph of a whole person that's been cut out.) For another, you can suspend the faces above the ground, then draw stems down from the faces into the ground, put a few leaves on the stems, and, presto, the faces are now flowers.

If the kids want, they can caption their pictures. The one of the balloons might be read, WHAT A WILD BUNCH OUR FAMILY IS. But the captions are strictly optional. The important thing is to combine the photos with crayons, markers, or paints, completing the picture with these other media better than the camera did.

Sandcasting

Materials needed: sand, shoebox or roasting pan or similarly sized container, water, "sleeve" of tagboard or posterboard or similar, plaster of paris, paper clip

If Grandma has a square inch of wall space not already given to pictures, drawings, art projects, and other grandchild memorabilia, a sandcasted print can be a genuinely treasured memento. Better yet, get your child or children to do several— there'll come a time when you yourself will treasure an impression of the four-year-old version of the handprint of your now-six-foot-two college linebacker.

If you don't have sand available from a sandbox, beach, or nearby riverbank, check with a local construction company or concrete contractor. They should be able to supply you. You only need enough sand to put a couple of inches' depth in a shoebox or other container. When you have the sand in a shoebox, roasting pan, large frying pan, or similar-sized container, wet the sand. You want it just wet enough that it doesn't break down or sag after it has an impression pressed into it. But don't make it so wet that it gets runny or too liquidlike to maintain a clean, clear impression.

Press your child's hand or bare foot—or your pet's paw—into the sand just enough to make an impression. (Is this the source of the expression, "Make a good impression on Grandma"?) Now cut a "sleeve" of tagboard, posterboard, or light cardboard, and place it around the impression. The purpose of the sleeve is to contain the plaster when you pour it. So the size you make it determines how large the plaster hanging will be when it's finished.

Ideally, the sleeve, which needn't be tall, should encompass an area about an inch or so out from the impression. Don't make the sleeve too large, or you'll have an unnecessarily large (and heavy) casting, and a lot of "dead space" around the impression. If placing the sleeve in position disturbs the impression, try pressing the hand or foot or whatever back into the sand, this time with the sleeve in position.

Prepare the plaster of paris. Don't mix more than you need, since there's no way to preserve it once you've mixed it. Pour the liquid mixture into the sand impression, letting it overflow the actual print and fill the space surrounded by the sleeve.

Before the plaster has cured (hardened) completely, put a paper clip into the plaster, bending it so it will be firmly embedded in the back of the medallion and can serve as a hook by which the casting can be hung on a wall. It's also a good idea to scratch the name of the handprint's maker, and the date.

Rock Face Paperweights

Materials needed: smooth, flat rocks or stones, paint, yarn, glue

You don't need to be terribly artistic to paint faces on rocks or stones to create interesting paperweights. Here's a project anyone in the family can get in on, even if they have no particular artistic abilities. Start with a rock or stone that's fairly smoothly contoured and has a reasonably flat shape, rather than being chunky.

Paint the face on, then glue pieces of yellow, brown, black, red, or even grey yarn above the face, as hair, and you have yourself a rock face suitable for use as a paperweight, or simply a decoration for a bookcase, shelf, or other surface. You can even create whole "families" of paperweights, using rocks or stones of comparable but slightly varying sizes.

Advice for Parents - Fun For Kids

The Caregiver's Manual: A Guide to Helping the Elderly and Infirm by Gene B. Williams & Patie Kay paperback $14.95 (#51597)

Children's Letters to Santa Claus, Compiled by Bill Adler hardcover $9.95 (#72196)

Creative Family Projects: Exciting and Practical Activities You Can Do Together by Cynthia MacGregor paperback $9.95 (#51636)

Cults: What Parents Should Know by Joan Carol Ross, Ed.M. & Michael D. Lange, Ph.D. paperback $5.95 (#40511)

The Day Care Kit : A Parent's Guide to Finding Quality Child Care by Deborah Spaide paperback $7.95 (#72031)

Getting Straight A's by Gordon W. Green, Jr., Ph.D. paperback $9.95 (#40571)

Great Videos For Kids: A Parent's Guide to Choosing the Best by Catherine Cella paperback $7.95 (#51377)

Grown Up Children, Grown Up Parents: Opening the Door to Healthy Relationships Between Parents and Adult Children by Phyllis Lieber, Gloria S. Murphy, and Annette Merkur Schwartz hardcover $18.95 (#72243)

Helping Your Child to Learn by Gordon W. Green, Jr., Ph.D. paperback $9.95 (#51497)

Helping Your Child to Learn Math by Gordon W. Green, Jr., Ph.D. paperback $10.95 (#51613)

How to be a Pregnant Father by Peter Mayle; illustrated by Arthur Robins paperback $9.95 (#40399)

How to Solve Your Child's Reading Problems by Ricki Linksman paperback $12.95 (#51618)

Kids' Book of Baseball: Hitting, Fielding, and the Rules of the Game by Godfrey Jordan paperback $8.95 (#51620)

Kids' Letters From Camp, Edited by Bill Adler hardcover $9.95 (#72226)

Kids Pick the Best Videos for Kids by Evan Levine paperback $9.95 (#51498)

Maybe You Know My Kid: A Parent's Guide to Identifying, Understanding and Helping Your Child With Attention Deficit Hyperactivity Disorder by Mary Fowler paperback $12.95 (#72209)

Mother Knows Best?: The Truth About Mom's Well-Meaning (but not always accurate) Advice by Sue Castle paperback $8.95 (#51631)

The Reading Rainbow Guide to Children's Books by Twila C. Liggett, Ph.D. and Cynthia Mayo Benfield; Introduction by LeVar Burton paperback $12.95 (#51493)

The Santa Claus Book by Alden Perkes paperback $14.95 (#40381)

Teaching Your Kids to Care: How to Discover and Develop the Spirit of Charity in Your Children by Deborah Spaide paperback $9.95 (#51637)

Upside Down Tales: Two books in one-- a classic children's tale, and an alternative, amusing version that sets the record straight!
Hansel & Gretel/The Witch's Story by Sheila Black Illustrated by Arlene Klemushin paperback $8.95 (#51520)
Jack & The Beanstalk/The Beanstalk Incident by Tim Paulson; illustrated by Mark Corcoran paperback $8.95 (#51313)
Little Red Riding Hood/The Wolf's Tale by Della Rowland; Illustrated by Michael Montgomery paperback $8.95 (#51526)
The Untold Story of Cinderella by Russell Shorto; illustrated by T. Lewis paperback $8.95 (#51298)

"What's Happening to Me?" by Peter Mayle; illustrated by Arthur Robins paperback $8.95 (#40312)

"Where Did I Come From?" by Peter Mayle; illustrated by Arthur Robins paperback $9.95 (#40253)

"Why Am I Going to Hospital?" by Claire Ciliotta & Carole Livingston; illustrated by Dick Wilson paperback $8.95 (#40568)

"Why Was I Adopted?" by Carole Livingston; illustrated by Arthur Robins paperback $8.95 (#40400)